DOGOPEDIA

a compendium of

CANINE CURIOSITIES

— FROM —

BATTERSEA

DOGS & CATS HOME

WITH JUSTINE HANKINS

headline

First published in 2015
by HEADLINE PUBLISHING GROUP

First published in paperback in 2016
by HEADLINE PUBLISHING GROUP

1

Cataloguing in Publication Data is available from the British Library

Paperback ISBN 978 1 4722 3778 1

Designed by Ben Cracknell

Illustrations by Laura Hall

Printed and bound in Great Britain by Clays Ltd, St Ives plc

Produced under licence from Battersea Dogs Home Ltd.
R Battersea Dogs & Cats Home.

Royalties from the sale of this book go towards supporting the
work of Battersea Dogs & Cats Home. Reg charity no: 206394

Battersea Dogs & Cats Home has been caring for and rehoming abandoned,
stray and neglected animals since 1860. We have looked after 3 million dogs
and cats since then and we aim never to turn away an animal in need of our help.
To find out more about the charity visit Battersea.org.uk

Headline's policy is to use papers that are natural, renewable and
recyclable products and made from wood grown in sustainable forests.
The logging and manufacturing processes are expected to conform to the
environmental regulations of the country of origin.

HEADLINE PUBLISHING GROUP
An Hachette UK Company
Carmelite House
50 Victoria Embankment
London EC4Y 0DZ
www.headline.co.uk
www.hachette.co.uk

Battersea Dogs & Cats Home has been caring for and rehoming abandoned, stray and neglected animals since 1860. We have looked after over three million dogs and cats since then, and we aim never to turn away an animal in need of our help. To find out more about our charity visit battersea.org.uk

Justine Hankins is a freelance journalist who has been writing about dogs for over fifteen years. A former Pets Editor of the *Guardian*, she now contributes to a variety of publications including Dogs Today, for which she has written a breed history column since 2002. Justine has four canine companions of her own: two miniature dachshunds, a toy poodle and a Portuguese podengo, all of whom contributed, in their own special way, to the writing of this book.

Acknowledgements

Many thanks to Conor Goold,
whose expertise and enthusiasm for all things
canine have been invaluable, and to the staff at
Battersea Dogs & Cats Home for their help in
compiling this book.

Justine Hankins, AUGUST 2015

CONTENTS

INTRODUCTION

In 1860, when she rented a disused stableyard to open what would one day become the world-famous Battersea Dogs & Cats Home, Mrs Mary Tealby made a solemn promise: she would never turn away an animal in need. That's a promise the Home still aims to keep today, over 3.1m dogs and cats later.

In 2014, Battersea looked after more than 8,000 lost, unwanted and abandoned animals, giving them a place of safety and the highest standards of care and welfare until a loving new home could be found.

In an uncertain world, one thing's for sure – our dogs love us unconditionally, and they deserve our care and respect. We've been companions for many thousands of years and the relationship looks as solid as ever. Like all good relationships, though, it needs to be worked at, mostly by us humans. Here's how we're doing so far...

Battersea's vision is of a world where every dog and cat has a safe and loving home. It rescues, reunites and rehomes – and also works hard to educate the public about responsible pet ownership, including microchipping, neutering and training.

The Home has three rehoming centres – in south London, at Brands Hatch in Kent, and at Old Windsor in Berkshire.

BATTERSEA'S HISTORY

1860 – The Temporary Home for Lost & Starving Dogs is set up by Mrs Mary Tealby in a disused stableyard in Holloway, North London

1871 – The Temporary Home moves to a new site in Battersea, where it has remained ever since

1883 – Battersea starts taking in cats

1885 – Queen Victoria becomes the Home's first royal patron

1898 – Due to a rabies epidemic in London the Duke and Duchess of Portland open the Home's first country site in Hackbridge, Surrey (now closed)

1911 – The Home starts collecting stray dogs from London police stations

1914 – 100 sledge dogs are housed at the Hackbridge site in preparation for Ernest Shackleton's second Antarctic Expedition

1917 – Dogs from Battersea make up the first batch of recruits of the War Dog School, and train to become messengers, sentries and munitions carriers in World War One

1956 – Queen Elizabeth II becomes the Home's patron

1960 – Battersea celebrates its centenary

1979 – Battersea acquires Bell Mead Kennels on the edge of Old Windsor

1998 – The BBC films the first of four documentary series on the Home

1990 – Battersea pioneers the microchipping of dogs, a system which has now become widespread and will be a legal requirement for all dogs in England from April 2016

2000 – Battersea's third centre, at Brands Hatch in Kent, is opened

2002 – The name changes to Battersea Dogs & Cats Home

2012 – The first series of ITV's behind the scenes at Battersea programme, *Paul O'Grady: For the Love of Dogs*, is screened, and a number of other series and Christmas Specials would follow.

2015 – Her Majesty The Queen officially opens Battersea's Mary Tealby kennels at the London centre.

IN WOLF'S CLOTHING

How the wolf came in from the cold

The domestic dog shares an astonishing 99.96% of its DNA with the grey wolf. This doesn't necessarily mean that modern dogs are directly descended from wolves exactly like the ones around today, it's more that the two species have a common ancestor. In other words, they're the kind of distant relatives who like to get a card but don't expect a present. Yet exactly how, when, where and why *Canis lupus* became our best friend is still the stuff of furious debate amongst scientists. Despite our familiarity with the pet dog, there's still a great deal we don't know about how wolves originally worked their way into our affections to become the first ever domesticated species.

WERE WOLVES INVITED INTO OUR HOMES, OR DID THEY GATECRASH?

Humans are not very good at domesticating animals. Indeed, throughout the whole of human history, the number of mammal species that have been truly domesticated (as opposed to just tame enough to keep in captivity without too many people getting bitten, kicked, scratched or pecked at) is barely in double figures. It's not for want of trying. The ancient Egyptians, in particular, had a go at domesticating all sorts of things, from gazelles to hyenas – but most of their efforts resulted in failure. So how come horses were domesticated, but not zebras? Why wolves but not their close relative, the coyote?

The truth is, we don't really know the answers to these questions. Humans and wolves had co-existed for hundreds of thousands of years, largely keeping out of each other's way. Then along came the dog. So what changed? Was it us or was it them? The domestication of the dog remains something of a riddle and current theories fall very roughly into two main camps: one is that the process of domestication was initiated by humans. The other is that wolves were the ones to make the first move. The first hypothesis suggests that humans adopted individual wolf cubs as pets (still today it's common for people in certain societies to take all manner of wild animals into their homes). Being raised by humans from a very young age made these animals more accepting and less fearful of people.

DOGTIONARY CORNER

Wolf, v. /wolf/ To wolf something down means to eat ravenously and probably without much concern for table manners.

Gradually, if this hypothesis is on the money, these tamer dogs bred with each other, ultimately creating a friendlier version of the wolf.

Followers of the second theory hold that this scenario is unlikely because it's not very easy to tame a wolf cub. Researchers working with wolves today have raised cubs exclusively in human company from about two weeks of age. This involves many hours of interaction and socialisation and has still not resulted in a wolf you'd be happy to take to the park. Even when raised with humans, wolf cubs grow up to be wolves – not dogs. This leads to the self-domestication hypothesis.

According to this version of events, as humans began to form settlements they created rubbish dumps near their homes, providing wolves, who are natural scavengers, with a handy larder. Very fearful animals who ran away at the slightest hint of human activity would not thrive in this environment – making willingness to be near humans, which we often call tameness, a successful survival strategy. Eventually, as with the previous hypothesis, this results in tame wolves producing young who are happy to approach humans. These youngsters then grow up to produce even more friendly canines until eventually they turn into something that's not quite a wolf anymore, but a dog.

Some researchers now believe there's probably a bit of truth in both theories. The domestication of the wolf was not a single event but a process which occurred over time and in more than one place. It could be that the dog is neither the result of purely human skill nor entirely the outcome of animal cunning, but a process of mutual development and adaptation with some random genetic changes thrown in.

No doubt further research will uncover more clues, particularly now scientists have the dog genome mapped out, but we may never get to the bottom of exactly how the modern domesticated dog as we know it came to be.

Ten characteristics our dogs share with wolves

1. The DNA of wolves and dogs is very nearly identical.

2. Both species are highly social animals.

3. Both wolves and dogs have 42 teeth.

4. Both animals paw the ground and circle before settling down.

5. Wolves and dogs both mark their territory by urinating at strategic points.

6. Both are omnivores and can adapt to a varied diet.

7. Wolves and dogs both lick their lips as a gesture of appeasement.

8. Captive-raised wolves have a similar life expectancy to dogs – around 10–18 years.

9. Both species can adapt to life in most ecological environments.

10. Wolf cubs and dog puppies develop their senses at the same age.

DOG LATIN

The Latin name for the wolf is *Canis Lupus*. There is no dispute about this, but what is the dog's taxonomic moniker? This question isn't so easy to answer. Sometimes the domestic dog is labelled *Canis lupus familiaris* – in other words, a subspecies of the wolf. Other experts prefer *Canis familiaris* – which suggests the dog is a species in its own right. Dogs and wolves can actually interbreed and produce fertile young, although most dog-wolf hybrids have come about through human intervention and dogs and wolves would not normally mate. It's a common oversimplification to assume that if animals can successfully reproduce they belong to the same species. Other factors also have to be taken into account, including habitat and behaviour – and there's no denying that wolves and dogs have very different lifestyles.

HOW TO TAME YOUR CANID

Selectively breeding for tameness can trigger physical changes in a process which may explain how dogs came about. At least that's the conclusion drawn from the work of pioneering Russian geneticist Dimitry Belyaev.

Belyaev began his experiments while working as a scientist at a silver fox fur farm in the Soviet Union in the 1950s and continued to the end of his life in 1985. His plan was to selectively breed for tameness to make the foxes easier to handle. He started with 30 male foxes and 100 vixens and evaluated them in a series of tests conducted when they were between one and seven months of age. The foxes were assessed according to their willingness to approach and be handled by humans and were divided into three categories. The most fearful or aggressive foxes were class III, class II foxes would tolerate touching but showed no inclination to approach people, and class I foxes were friendly towards their handlers. When foxes from this last group were bred together they produced a new class in only a few generations – class IE, the domesticated elite. These foxes not only tolerated handling but actively sought out attention by whimpering and sniffing and licking their handlers.

None of these animals were raised by humans in the way a puppy would be – they lived in cages and had relatively little direct contact with people. The animals involved in the experiment were selected on the basis of one single behavioural trait – tameness, or reduced fear response – but within the relatively short evolutionary period of under 30 years which produced forty generations, a number of unanticipated physical changes began to occur as well. Some of the foxes had multi-coloured or piebald coats, floppy ears, curly tails, smaller skulls and shorter muzzles – all characteristics found in domestic dogs.

Belyaev's research showed that selecting for one trait can cause a chain of random and unexpected morphological changes. It's possible that something similar happened to wolves – as they either became tamer or were made tamer by selective breeding they started to undergo the physical transformation from wolf to dog.

FOREVER YOUNG

Ever wondered why your dog is so cute? Well it's partly down to a phenomenon known as domestication syndrome – the term used by scientists to describe the retention of juvenile traits into adulthood. Most domestic animals keep some of their baby features when they become adults, but domestication syndrome is particularly apparent in dogs, especially in certain breeds. Juvenile features include a large head and eyes and floppy ears. Adult dogs are also more playful than adult wolves and retain wolf cub behaviours such as licking faces. These juvenile features seem to be particularly appealing to humans, probably because we have a strong instinct to nurture youngsters (babies, like puppies, have big heads and eyes). Dogs are the Peter Pans of the canine world – the wolves that wouldn't grow up.

WHEN DID DOMESTICATION OCCUR?

Carbon dating of archaeological remains suggests that domestic dogs have existed for somewhere around 12,000 to 14,000 years. That's long before any other species was brought into the human fold (sheep hold the number two position, having been domesticated in around 8500 BC). Ancient dog skeletons have been found at various sites around the world including Europe, North America, the Middle East and China, suggesting that domestic dogs became widespread at the time humans began to develop agriculture and permanent settlements.

Until a decade or so ago, this was all we had to go on – but then along came the DNA revolution. In the 1990s, an international team of scientists sequenced the DNA of dogs and wolves and came to the astonishing conclusion that the dog and wolf became separate species about 100,000 years ago. They arrived at this calculation by comparing the mitochondrial DNA (mtDNA) of dogs and wolves. mtDNA are chains of DNA outside the cell nucleus (where most DNA is found) and passed on through the mother's genes. Over time, mutations occur in the mtDNA and the rate of these mutations is believed to be constant, effectively acting as a 'clock' that becomes a useful tool for analysing the evolutionary relationships between different species.

Subsequent studies have questioned this timeframe and new estimates have been put forward suggesting that domestication occurred somewhere between 15,000 and 40,000 years ago. There's still no archaeological proof that dogs are this old, but that doesn't mean the DNA evidence is wrong, it's just that the canine genome is still very much a work in progress and old dog bones are hard to find. New research is going on all the time, which will no doubt continue to challenge what we know about dogs, their domestication and their divergence from their wolf ancestors.

PAW PRINTS IN THE ARDÈCHE

One of the oldest pieces of physical evidence of humans and canines sharing living space is some footprints found in the Chauvet-Pont-D'Arc cave in the Ardèche region of France. This cave is famous for its remarkably well-preserved paintings, which date back around 26,000 years, but it also contains another fascinating find. There is a set of footprints, apparently made by a small child, right next to some large canine paw prints. Could the latter be a wolf, or a dog? Was the wolf/dog a companion of the child? Were the prints made together or on separate occasions, possibly hundreds of years apart? This intriguing discovery leaves many questions unanswered but there's no doubt that people and dog-like animals have been crossing paths for a very long time.

THE MYSTERY OF THE AIN MALLAHA PUPPY

An elderly person of indeterminate sex lying with a hand resting on a puppy. This was the remarkable find at a Natufian settlement in what is now Israel. The Natufians were among the first people to establish permanent settlements in the eastern Mediterranean region and the pair were buried together around 12,000 years ago. One can only guess at why they were buried in the same tomb or why someone so carefully placed the hand on the puppy in a gesture which looks to us like affection.

DIGGING UP OLD BONES

Given that dogs and wolves share many physical similarities, how do archaeologists know if they've unearthed a very old wolf or a really early dog? Solving this puzzle is crucial to working out when wolves became dogs, but the difficulty of separating the wolves from the dogs has sometimes been a barrier to identifying when and where domestic dogs first appeared. Archaeologists look for clues such as shorter muzzles and smaller teeth, which suggest dogs rather than wolves, but when you've only got a few bones to go on it can be difficult to identify which species is which. Many dogs, for instance, have shorter forelimbs than wolves, but some have longer legs. On top of that, wolves have also changed over the ages and they may have once been smaller – dog-size, in fact – making it difficult to know whose humerus you're looking at.

Ten reasons why our dogs are not wolves

1. Dogs bark far more often and in a greater variety of situations than wolves, who tend to reserve this form of vocalisation for occasional warnings.

2. Dog hair sheds all year round, while wolves only shed their coats in the spring.

3. Dogs become sexually mature earlier than wolves and come into season twice a year, whereas wolves usually mate only in the winter for a spring litter.

4. Dogs seek out eye contact with humans as a way of gathering information about what's going on. Wolves avoid eye contact with each other and with people.

5. Dogs are highly social but they're not true pack animals; while they hunt and scavenge alongside each other, they don't hunt co-operatively like wolves.

6. Dogs have a much wider range of coat colour and pattern than wolves, including patches, splotches, dots, two-colour, tri-colour, merle (patches) and brindle (stripes) – features rarely seen in wolves.

7. Dogs are poor hunters compared to wolves; although humans have bred many types of hunting dogs, what they actually do in most cases is find, chase or retrieve the prey.

8. Puppies have a later window of socialisation than wolf cubs, so they learn about and form an attachment to humans when their senses are more fully developed.

9. Dogs are open to friendly encounters with new dogs and people throughout their lives; adult wolves, even when reared by humans, are generally hostile to strangers.

10. Dogs have smaller skulls and brains than wolves, but there's no consensus on whether this also means reduced intelligence.

WILD DOGS

Meet the relatives

Dogs are members of the *Canidae* family, which includes wolves, foxes, jackals and coyotes. There are at least 34 canid species living in the world today and they are largely social animals who can adapt to a wide range of habitats, diets and lifestyles. Canids also tend to be opportunistic, as any dog owner who's turned their back on a chicken sandwich will know.

Canis familiaris – our very own canine companion – has arguably shown the greatest degree of behavioural flexibility, which is why there are roughly 500 million companion dogs in the world today. The total domestic dog population could be up to one billion if you include all the free-ranging dogs as well as pets. The urban fox, the suburban coyote and the city jackal are also quick to take advantage of opportunities thrown their way and thrive in different environments around the world. Unfortunately, not all members of the Canidae family are so lucky and some are seriously under threat from habitat loss and human persecution.

...AND ONE CASE OF MISTAKEN IDENTITY

Although hyenas look a bit dog-like and hang round in groups like dogs, they are actually more closely related to felines than canines and are officially classified as Feliformia – cat-like carnivores.

Ten species of the Canidae family...

1. Side-striped jackal (*Canis adustus*): This woodland dwelling jackal lives in central and southern Africa and eats small mammals, scavenged prey and fruit.

2. Golden jackal (*Canis aureus*): This wide-ranging omnivore lives in northern Africa, the Middle East, India and parts of south-east Asia and southern Europe.

3. Ethiopian wolf (*Canis simensis*): This endangered canid requires a highly specialised diet and environment and it's believed there are only around 500 living in the wild.

4. Black-backed jackal (*Canis mesomelas*): This jackal has a distinct stripe on its back and is a keen hunter. Its range includes southern and eastern Africa.

5. Coyote (*Canis latrans*): The American coyote has a wide range from Panama in the south to Alaska in the north and thrives in and around urban areas.

6. African wild dog (*Lycaon pictus*): This endangered dog with a distinctive patterned coat is highly social and lives in large packs of up to 30 adults.

7. Dhole (*Cuon alpinus*): Sometimes known as the Asian red dog, this canid lives in social groups, hunting medium or even large animals such as wild boar or buffalo.

8. Short-eared dog (*Atelocynus microtis*): This elusive species lives in the Amazon region of south America and doesn't live in close proximity to human settlements.

9. Maned wolf (*Chrysocyon Brachyurus*): This long-legged wolf from South America is the tallest wild canid and usually hunts alone.

10. Raccoon dog *(Nyctereutes procyonides)*: This curious east Asian canid climbs trees, looks very much like a raccoon and is the only canid known to hibernate.

THE UNUSUAL NATURAL HISTORY OF THE DINGO

The dingo is as closely associated with Australia as the kangaroo or the koala, yet this dog from Oz is not actually an Australian native. The oldest fossil remains of a dingo found in Australia date back to around 1500 BC, although it's believed that they arrived some time before that – possibly four to five thousand years ago.

But what is the dingo exactly? Is it a type of wolf, a sub-species in its own right, or just a domestic pet turned wild? It has been variously described as all of these but the general consensus now is that the dingo's ancestors were domestic dogs taken to the island by Asian seafarers. Domesticated, but left to their own devices in the new land, these dogs had to learn to fend for themselves. So dingoes are not wild but feral.

What marks dingoes out from other feral dogs, however, is that they have thrived in the wild, independently of humans – which is why they are sometimes classified as a wild species. Most free-ranging dogs around the world are dependent on people and hang round human settlements rummaging through rubbish and begging for snacks. The dingo, by contrast, had the great fortune to arrive on an island with no large predators (indeed, the dingo is the largest predator species in Australia) and a range of small, tasty mammals with few inbuilt defence mechanisms to match this unfamiliar predator. The dingo quickly adapted to life down under and ranged across the whole of mainland Australia.

Of course, there were already humans in Australia and indigenous Australians have long been associated with the dingo (in fact the dog's name comes from a word which means 'tame dog' in one of the Aboriginal languages). Dingoes are a common subject in Aboriginal myth, art and folklore, but the extent to which they were either tame or useful is unclear. Research suggests that Aboriginal people often took in puppies but these cute youngsters tended to become destructive or disruptive on reaching adulthood and took themselves back to the wild. As far as hunting was concerned, the dingo seems to have been more of a hindrance than a help.

Wild or tame, useful or not, the dingo was given a great deal of respect in Aboriginal culture. But the fortunes of this primitive dog were to take a turn for the worse with the arrival of European settlers in the late 18th century. As the new arrivals began farming, the dingo was seen as a threat to livestock and numbers declined dramatically due to persecution and habitat loss. More recently, the greatest threat to the survival of the dingo as a unique species actually comes from other dogs. Because the dingo is genetically, biologically, physiologically and every other way just a dog, they can interbreed with domestic dogs with ease. Indeed, it's thought that up to 80 per cent of dingoes today are hybrids. Moves to support the conservation of 'pure' dingoes may be too little too late.

THE NEW GUINEA SINGING DOG

This little-known relative of the dingo is quite possibly the rarest dog on earth. These cat-like creatures can climb trees and get their name from their distinctive howling, which sounds like a cross between a wolf and whale, if you can imagine such a thing, particularly when they sing in chorus.

Like the dingo, the Singer – as they are sometimes known – is descended from domestic dogs but because of its remote habitat on the island of New Guinea has remained isolated from other dog populations and is regarded as one of the most primitive dog in existence. These dogs are critically endangered and it's uncertain how many remain in the wild. A photograph of what is believed to be a New Guinea Singing Dog was taken by trekkers on an expedition to New Guinea in 2012 – a rare piece of evidence of this seldom seen canine.

MY FAMILY COMPANION
AND OTHER CANINES

Dogs live within or alongside nearly every human society in the world but the nature of their interaction with people varies widely. Researchers who study dogs have come up with a number of terms to describe the different social circumstances that dogs can find themselves in. Our family pets are 'owned' dogs, which describes a dog belonging to one particular household. There are also strays, which are generally owned dogs who have become lost or been abandoned.

Most of the world's dogs are neither of these but co-exist alongside humans in a sometimes uneasy coalition. These are the dogs that survive on the fringes of human society by scavenging and begging; the dogs you see on beaches in Thailand, on the streets of Indian cities or hanging around African villages. Researchers recognise a formal distinction between dogs that don't depend on humans (feral dogs) and 'free-ranging dogs', a term which describes the millions of dogs in the world who are not attached to any one individual but are, nevertheless, often dependent on human society to some extent.

DOGTIONARY CORNER

Whelp, v. & n. /hwɛlp/ As a noun, the word 'whelp' is an Old English word meaning 'young dog' and has now largely been replaced by 'puppy'. The verb is still used to describe the action of giving birth when it applies to dogs and similar animals.

DOG'S BODY

The remarkable physiology of the domestic dog

Dogs come in all sorts of coat types, lots of different colours and a greater variety of shapes and sizes than any other species on earth, largely due to selective breeding. On top of that, dogs have important features that humans lack. A tail for a start, and an amazing set of nostrils. Although we share the same basic senses with dogs and other mammals, there are significant differences in how we perceive things. If we experienced the world the way our dogs do, it would be much less colourful, a bit more blurry, a lot noisier and considerably more pungent. We may be on the same walk with our dogs, but differences in our physiology make for a very different experience.

LOOK INTO MY EYES

It's not unusual for a dog owner to gaze lovingly into their dog's eyes, and at first glance they're not that different to our own – they are a similar shape and even size. On closer examination, however, there are some significant differences which mean that humans and dogs don't see eye to eye on what the world actually looks like.

Firstly, our eyes are right at the front of our faces, whereas dogs' eyes are slightly to the side, giving them a wider field of vision. Humans can see about 180 degrees but dogs have a more panoramic view of 240–270 degrees, depending on head shape. This means that dogs are better at seeing things out of the corner of their eye – all the better for spotting those small animals flitting about or potential enemies approaching.

Another key difference is that the human eye can do something called 'accommodation', which means the lens can change shape, allowing us to focus on things very close up. Dogs have much less capacity for this visual accommodation, so they are unable to focus on things that are right under their nose. We can focus on things as close as 7cm away (which is why you are able to read this book) whereas anything closer than about 30cm is all a blur to a dog, so they sniff it or stick it in their mouths to find out more about it.

Dogs do have a key advantage over us when it comes to eyesight, however; something called the *tapetum lucidum*. This is a reflective layer of cells behind the retina which boosts night vision and creates a glow in the dark look in dim light (and makes pets frustrating subjects of flash photography). There are other mammals with much better night vision than dogs, but humans lack the necessary equipment altogether.

EYES WHITE

The white of the eye – the sclera – is much more visible in humans than in dogs and most other mammals. This makes it easier to follow the direction of someone's gaze and work out what they are looking at. In addition to this, our pupils expand and contract depending not only on light levels but also on our emotions and state of arousal. We give ourselves away with our eyes much more than dogs but our instinct to read eyes is so strong that many of us are convinced we can read a whole range of complex emotions in a dog's gaze.

WHY THERE'S NO POINT GIVING YOUR DOG A COLOURING BOOK

As dogs don't have opposable thumbs, holding a felt-tip pen is a little tricky. But even if they could manage this, they still wouldn't make very good artists. One reason for this is that dogs can't focus on things close up (see previous page) but the major factor inhibiting your dog's inner Michelangelo is a little difficulty with colour.

Humans have three types of cones (cells in the retina which are sensitive to colour) which respond to red, green and blue. Dogs, on the other hand (along with most mammals), only have two types of cones, corresponding roughly to blue-violet and yellowish-green. Contrary to popular belief, a dog's vision is not limited to black and white, but while we can see a whole rainbow of shades in vivid glory, a dog's world is mainly blue, yellow and grey. Dogs have particular difficulty distinguishing the range of colours between red and green. A red ball on a green lawn might seem blindingly obvious to us, but your dog may not be able to make it out.

WHAT'S ON TELEVISION?

Just a load of old repeats? From your dog's point of view it's not so much a repeat as a constant flicker. Dogs are excellent at detecting movement but TV is just too slow for them. Television images are refreshed around 60 times a second. This is perfect for people, who need to see about 16 to 20 images a second for something to look like continuous movement. This is called the flicker fusion rate, and for humans it's around 55hz. Dogs, on the other hand, have a flicker fusion rate of 70–80hz, which means television probably just looks like a flickering, static image. Dogs often appear to be watching television, but they are most likely responding to the sounds they hear or are just curious about what it is that takes up so much of our time.

ALL EARS

Dogs can hear noises at ultrasound frequencies – that is, sounds too high for humans to hear (above about 20 kHz). The frequency range for humans is between 20 and 20,000 Hz compared to 40 to 60,000 Hz in dogs, so we can hear slightly more in the lower range, but dogs can hear significantly better in the higher range. Dogs don't make ultrasound noises themselves, but small rodents do. Being able to hear high-pitched squeaks is an obvious advantage to an animal on the lookout for a snack. This sensitivity to high-pitched noises may also be why dogs often react badly to vacuum cleaners, electric drills and other everyday sounds.

EAR WIGGLE

Dogs have very prominent ears compared to humans. Selective breeding has created dogs with all sorts of ear shapes, but if we let them get on with choosing their own mates, all dogs would eventually end up with pricked ears – like wolves. Other ear shapes come about because humans spot a variation they like and selectively breed for it. There are at least 18 muscles in the canine ear, making it much more mobile than our own (most people are unable to move their ears at will, although there's always someone with a party trick). Dogs can tilt, swivel, lower or prick up their ears – which makes them very good at identifying the direction a noise is coming from, and means they can identify the precise location of a sound much more quickly than humans.

A NOSE FOR IT: HOW DOGS SMELL

Smell is far and away the most important sense to dogs. They take in the world not primarily through their eyes, as we do, but through their nostrils. The canine world is an olfactory treasure trove where every street corner is a detailed message, every dog's rear-end is a biography and every item of our clothing is an information explosion. Dragging your dog away from that lamp post is like taking a person into a museum and then covering their eyes.

Dogs collect scent by either sniffing the air or the ground, a process assisted by a moist nose which enables molecules to stick to the nostrils and maximises scent detection. They can even control each nostril independently to identify which direction a smell is coming from. Like humans and many other animals, when a dog takes a sniff, molecules swirl around the nasal cavity and are processed by an olfactory bulb, sending messages to the brain. Inside the dog's nose is the olfactory epithelium – a layer of tissue involved in odour detection. In dogs, it is between 150–170 cm². In humans, by contrast, it is only about 5cm².

The canine olfactory epithelium is not only much bigger than the human version, it also contains far more scent receptor cells. Dogs have somewhere between 125 and 300 million scent receptors, depending on breed-type, compared to a paltry 5 million or so in humans.

Thanks to this superior nasal physiology, dogs can smell a lot more detail than people. Where we can smell soup, a dog can smell the onions, carrots, potatoes and stock cube as well as the sweat on the chef's T-shirt. They can also detect scents at far lower concentrations than people. Tests have shown that dogs can detect a chemical in a solution diluted to one to two parts per trillion – that's the equivalent of a spoonful of sugar in not one, but two Olympic-sized swimming pools.

[2 8]

VOMERONASAL ORGAN

Dogs, along with many other animals, have an auxiliary sense organ in the roof of the mouth known as the vomeronasal organ (VNO). This allows them to 'taste' smells. It's thought that the canine VNO can detect sex pheromones and may be used in social encounters, too.

HOT DOGS

Dogs do sweat, just not very effectively. They have sweat glands in their paw pads but that's not always enough to cool them down, which is why they may pant in hot weather and why it's potentially fatal to leave them in hot cars.

HOW LONG DO DOGS LIVE AND WHAT IS A 'DOG YEAR'?

How long is a 'dog year'? Seven human years is the figure that's often bandied about, although no one's really sure when or why people started talking about 'dog years'. This number, however, doesn't shed much light on which life stage our dogs are at. For a start, youth is fleeting, especially in animals. A one-year-old dog is not at the equivalent stage of development as a seven-year-old child. They can reproduce, for one thing, and have done most of their growing. One-year-old dogs are in fact more like teenagers in our species, so it makes more sense to calculate the first year of a dog's life as about 15 of our own. To complicate matters further, canine life expectancy varies significantly according to breed and size. Large breeds, such as Irish Wolfhounds and Mastiffs, can expect to live to about nine or ten, while some small breeds live well into their teens. In addition, there is evidence suggesting that mongrels generally live longer than pedigree dogs. On top of that, life expectancy in dogs is going up, just as with humans, thanks to better nutrition, medicine and care – so dogs living until the equivalent of their 80s or 90s are not as uncommon as they once were.

A slightly more sophisticated way of calculating your dog's age in human terms is to count the first two years as ten each (making a two-year-old dog equivalent to a 20-year-old person) and then count the rest as four. This is still a bit hit and miss as, by this calculation, a 12-year-old dog would be 60 in human years, which for some dogs might be about right, but for other dogs 12 is very old indeed. There are more sophisticated methods for coming up with a human age for your dog, but these invariably involve complicated sums and measuring your dog. In any case, all this mathematics isn't really necessary – giving dogs human ages serves little useful purpose so you might as well just count your dog's age using the same twelve-month calendar years we use for everything else.

DOGTIONARY CORNER

Bark, v. & n. /bɑːk/ Used to describe the noise that dogs and some other animals make, the word 'bark' first appeared in Old English as 'beorcan'. The word had changed to 'barke' by Shakespeare's time.

Ten breeds with unusual physical characteristics

1. Basenjis: Sometimes called 'the barkless dog', these African hounds actually yodel.

2. Dachshunds: These long-backed dogs have tiny legs because of a genetic mutation.

3. Chow Chows: These thick-coated Chinese dogs have a blue-black tongue.

4. Pharaoh Hounds: When excited, these sight hounds 'blush', with ears and nose turning rosy-pink.

5. Newfoundlands: With webbed feet, these giant dogs are swimming champions.

6. Poodles: The dense, curly coat of these dogs doesn't shed, but grows quickly and matts easily.

7. Komondors: These mop-like Hungarian herding dogs have a distinctive corded coat.

8. Xoloitzcuintlis: An ancient dog from Mexico, these dogs are naturally hairless.

9. Rhodesian Ridgebacks: The breed name refers to the ridge of hair growing 'the wrong way' down their backs.

10. Catalburuns – A rare Turkish breed with a highly unusual, naturally occurring split nose where a layer of skin separates the nostrils.

DOGS' BEHAVIOUR

Why our dogs do what they do

Even the most devoted dog person would find it hard to deny that dogs sometimes do some pretty bizarre things and that not all their habits are entirely pleasant. For example, the appeal of being covered in stinking fox poo is not immediately apparent to your average human. Nor are the attractions of drinking toilet water or sniffing a dog's bum. But, from a dog's point of view, everything they get up to makes perfect sense and the things we find the most baffling or disgusting can be the most fun. If dogs want to live happily with us, they have to accept some of our rules (no raiding the cat litter, for instance, and definitely no dead rabbits on the sofa) but the human-canine relationship can only be enriched by a better understanding of what motivates our dogs' behaviour.

BOW WOW WOW

Dogs may not be able to speak using anything remotely like a human language, but they're no strangers to vocal communication. As well as a number of different barks, dogs produce an astonishing range of noises, including yelping, yapping, growling, whining, snarling and, in some types of dogs, howling. Are they trying to tell us something?

Well, the first thing to note is that although barking is strongly associated with dogs, they are not the only animals to vocalise in this way. Other canids bark, as do other mammals such as monkeys, lemurs, squirrels and meerkats. Even birds do it. But dogs bark much more often than other animals and in a greater variety of situations. Almost anything can set them off – cats, other dogs, doorbells, buses, friends, family and strangers.

So why do dogs bark so much? One function of barking in wolves and other animals is to alert the rest of the group to the presence of an intruder – this is known as mobbing behaviour. This alarm calling is familiar to anyone who's visited a re-homing centre such as Battersea. The dogs may be perfectly quiet until someone enters the kennels. First one dog barks and pretty soon all the dogs have something to say for themselves. Domestic dogs are frequently faced with unfamiliar situations and have to deal with the constant coming and going that life with humans entails. On top of that, they are nearly always constrained in some way; in a garden or house or on a lead, making barking (rather than running away) their first line of defence. Researchers have noted that barking is less frequent in free-ranging and feral dogs – who have the option of staying well out of the way.

Of course, there's more to doggy-speak than just 'Watch out!'. Dogs also bark when they want to eat, play or go for a walk. This has led some researchers to speculate that the extensive vocal repertoire of the domestic dog is an adaptation caused by their long and close interaction with humans. In other words, barking may be about more than just an expression of an internal, emotional state (loneliness, say, or fear) and may be an attempt to communicate something about the external world ('open the back door', or 'next door's cat is in the garden').

So how effective are dogs at getting their message across? A number of studies have been carried out to find out whether humans can actually interpret different barks. People with and without dogs listen to recordings of barks and are asked to identify the mood of the dog. The results suggest that people can identify whether a dog is playful, aggressive or fearful just from the sound of their bark more reliably than would be expected by chance. The findings are by no means conclusive, but perhaps we are better than we thought at understanding what our dogs are trying to tell us.

WAG THE DOG

A wagging tail means a happy dog, right? Well, much of the time this is perfectly true. Dogs do relaxed wags, excited wags, pleased to see you wags and sometimes they're so happy they have to move their entire rear end to get a big enough tail wag. But dogs can also use their tails to issue a warning. If the body stiffens and the tail is raised high and shaken quickly like a flag in the wind, the dog could be showing aggression and saying 'stay away'. A low tail wag, especially when placed between the legs, could mean a dog is anxious and doesn't want to upset anyone.

Some researchers have observed that dogs move their tails slightly more to the right when they are happy, but if they feel threatened or stressed they wag more to the left. It seems that this message is not lost on other dogs, who react differently to right and left wagging. Scientists measured the heart rates of dogs as they encountered a strange dog and found that they showed signs of anxiety when meeting a left wagging dog but were more relaxed about a right wagger.

Human intervention has led to a wide variety of dog tail shapes; tails can be bob-tail, tufted, plumed, carrot-shaped, tapered, curled or kinked. Dogs do not need their tails for balance and movement as much as some other animals, such as cats or monkeys, although they may play a role as a counterbalance when dogs jump or make sharp turns. In some breeds they can be used as a rudder while swimming and sled dogs like to use their fluffy tails to keep their faces warm when they're curled up. Back in the long-distant, evolutionary past, dogs may have had more uses for their tails, but there's no doubt that the number one function of the modern dog's tail is communication.

AN INVITATION TO THE GAME

The play bow is often a dog's way of announcing to other dogs that they're not a threat and they just want to play. They rest on their front legs, chest close to the ground, bum in the air and tail held high and wagging. This is a distinctive characteristic of canine communication familiar to any dog owner. Less understood, perhaps, is that this gesture may also be used when a dog is feeling threatened. It's half-way between pouncing forward and running away. Wolves have been filmed doing play bows in front of bison, usually when one of these massive bovines is about to charge – it's safe to say they probably weren't looking for a playmate.

BIZARRE OBJECTS SWALLOWED BY DOGS

Battersea staff often have to deal with dogs with unusual things in their stomachs. Bull Mastiff cross Patrick, for instance, came in with a kebab skewer protruding from his side. Luckily, it had missed all his vital organs and Battersea vets were able to safely remove it. Another dog, Barney, produced two pairs of black cotton underpants and a black thong during his morning toilet walk. Fortunately, there was no permanent damage. A terrier called Alf was found with an iron nail driven through his bottom lip, possibly the result of careless gnawing through a wood pile. Battersea vets have also had to remove a toy bus, a corn on the cob and a squeaky toy from the stomachs of incautious canines.

I LOVE YOU, TOO – BUT THAT'S A BIT INAPPROPRIATE

There's no denying that many dogs enjoy mounting things: sometimes other dogs (of the opposite or the same gender), sometimes parts of people (especially legs), but often inanimate objects will do (pillows and toys are favourites). This behaviour might be explained away as sexual frustration in uncastrated adult males, but sometimes puppies, neutered males and females do it. The prevalence of what appears to be sexual mounting in dogs suggests that it might not actually be all about sex.

Some researchers believe that mounting is a dominance behaviour and it's also been observed that dogs are more likely to mount when they are excited or stressed. In some cases, it can be a compulsive behaviour, similar to excessive tail chasing. The truth is, we don't fully understand why dogs do this, although the common denominator seems to be some kind of physiological arousal caused by situations such as social competition or high-energy play. We do know, however, that it makes many owners feel extremely embarrassed. Of course, dogs are much more relaxed about this kind of thing so maybe we should be too.

DOGTIONARY CORNER

Yappy, adj. /'jæpɪ/ The onomatopoeic noun 'yap' has been used to suggest the noise dogs make since the 17th century. The adjective 'yappy' is mostly used to describe small dogs and is not usually complimentary.

DON'T MAKE ME YAWN

Tedium may induce yawning but there's nothing boring about the investigation into why yawning occurs. Dogs, like people, sometimes yawn because they're bored or tired, but there's more to it than that. They also seem to yawn to relieve stress and studies have shown that it lowers blood pressure and may reduce brain temperature, helping dogs (and people) to feel calm in tense situations.

It's long been observed that yawning in humans is contagious. Seeing someone else yawn, or even reading about it can induce involuntary yawning, although why this happens is not fully understood. Intriguingly, dogs also yawn when they see other dogs or people yawning. Contagious yawning has also been observed in Chimpanzees but not in other animals.

Studies have shown that up to 70% of dogs will yawn in response to a yawning researcher or even the sound of someone yawning. One study suggests that dogs are more likely to 'catch' their owner's yawn than that of a complete stranger, leading some to conclude that collective yawning has a social function and may be an indication of empathy.

Contagious yawns may also perform the dual functions connected to 'fight or flight' as a habit which evolved in groups where one drowsy individual's yawn would spread through the group as the others copy it in order to stay alert in the face of predators. The same yawns could be used by groups of animals to indicate that all is well and it is safe to sleep.

Ten odd things that dogs do explained

1. **Scooting:** this is when dogs drag their bottoms along the floor, which may leave unfortunate marks on the carpet. There are two main reasons why dogs do this – one is to relieve itchy or infected anal sacs and the other is because they have worms. Nobody looks forward to dealing with anal sacs, but sometimes it has to be done.

2. **Crotch-sniffing:** From a dog's point of view there's nothing impolite about having a good old sniff of the personal parts when you meet someone new. This is, after all, how they introduce themselves to each other. For quite a few dogs, the human crotch is about head height, making it the perfect source of information about a new acquaintance.

3. **Eating poo:** Dogs are not known for their refined eating habits but scoffing faeces is perhaps their least appealing activity. Horse manure is popular, as are rabbit droppings when the opportunity arises, and cat poo is a real favourite. Some dogs even eat their own waste. Humans may be horrified, but dogs rarely come to any harm from this behaviour, although they are at risk from worms and it may indicate an unbalanced diet.

4. **Snapping at the air:** Some dogs snap and bite at what appears to be nothing in particular as if they are trying to catch an insect. If excessive, it can indicate an obsessive-compulsion.

5. **Rolling in smelly things:** Dog walkers dread discovering their companion joyously rolling in something potently pungent like fox poo or a recently deceased rabbit, but dogs are just fulfilling an ancestral instinct. Dogs probably like to disguise themselves in these scents because this camouflage made it easier for them to hunt when they had to find their own food. Dogs also tend to roll in something rotten when they've just been bathed – they're not as keen as smelling of floral fragrances as we are.

6. **Chewing up things you really care about:** Dogs don't deliberately choose your favourite pair of shoes or your brand-new mobile phone to chew, it's just that those are the things you notice the most. Chewing is a normal part of the way puppies explore their world but in older dogs it can indicate boredom, not to mention the fact that their owners don't tidy their things away carefully enough.

7. **Chasing cars:** It seems natural for dogs to chase small furry things or substitutes such as balls and Frisbees, but why do some dogs chase cars or other vehicles? Any moving object can trigger a chase response and dogs may develop a habit for chasing cars because their efforts are also successful – the 'intruder' car always goes away.

8. **Eating grass:** A lot of people believe that dogs only eat grass because they need to be sick. There may be some truth in this idea that grass induces vomiting and soothes an upset stomach, but the fact is nobody really knows for sure why dogs do this. They may be missing some nutrients in their diet or they could just enjoy the taste.

9. **Swallowing non-food objects:** Some dogs eat fabric, some prefer electronic items and some dine on rubber bands or plastic bags. Dogs, especially puppies, often put anything and everything in their mouths, but actually eating non-edible items is a condition known as pica, which has a number of causes and can have serious consequences if not treated.

10. **Licking human mouths:** Some dog owners like to think that mouth licks are equivalent to human kisses and are a sign of affection. Well, yes and no. It's not really a kiss but it might suggest familial closeness. Wolf cubs lick their mothers around the mouth as a prompt to feeding and puppies are also really big on face licking. Licking may also be one of the many, many ways your dog has of getting your attention.

FIGHTING LIKE CATS AND DOGS

If cartoons were your only source of information about the world you'd be convinced that dogs and cats are sworn enemies, destined to a perpetual scrap. Happily, dogs and cats can live together harmoniously, but there's no denying the fur sometimes flies when these two animals encounter each other. It's not always so much dislike as a misunderstanding. Although some dogs may regard cats as prey animals like any other, dogs often actually like cats very much indeed, so much so that they become over-excited – behaviour which cats tend to find very uncouth. The trouble is dogs and cats generally don't share the same play styles, which can get them off on the wrong foot. The way cats move, for example, can trigger a dog's chase instinct, and no cat wants to be chased up and down the garden.

Some dogs are less annoying than others from a cat's point of view, depending on breed type and individual temperament. Dogs that are raised with cats when they are puppies are more likely to be able to keep their cool around cats. Battersea dogs can be 'cat tested' to assess how suitable they are for co-habitation with a feline friend. Dog-tolerant cats are introduced to the dog at a safe distance and in a controlled, safe environment so staff can observe the dog's reaction.

POSTMAN'S KNOCK

Postal workers, like cats, are traditionally viewed as objects of canine hatred. Many dogs launch into a tirade of barking every single day just because a person is going about their job. From the dog's point of view, it's not hatred at all – it's just an extremely successful strategy. The person who brings the post is a potential intruder, just like any other, so it's only right to warn your owner that something untoward might be happening. Every time this happens, the person goes away – danger averted, job done.

SCENT MAIL

Dogs seem to really, really enjoy peeing. They pee on lamp-posts, trees, walls, clumps of leaves and bags of rubbish that they pass on their walks. Leg-cocking is most associated with male dogs, but females will sometimes have a go, too, balancing on three legs and raising their rear end as high as possible before giving a little squirt.

These pee-mails contain urine as well as strong-smelling secretions from the anal sac (the same delightful aroma dogs enjoy sniffing on each other). Interestingly, dogs kept penned up on their own don't scent mark anywhere near as often – suggesting the purpose of this behaviour is primarily to communicate with other dogs. They nearly always sniff before they pee, so this is a two-way conversation. But what are they saying to each other with these urinary messages?

Dogs can probably tell how old the message is, as well as the sex and size of the other dog (some dogs try to get their message as high as they can, possibly to make themselves seem bigger to the next passing dog). Studies have shown that dogs tend to investigate the urine of unfamiliar

DOGTIONARY CORNER

Doggy bag, n. /ˈdɒgibæg/ The first recorded usage of this term comes from 1950s America, when some restaurants started offering the service of a take-home bag for leftover food which could be given to a dog. Nowadays, food taken home in a doggy bag is just as likely to be consumed by a person as a dog.

dogs in more detail than familiar ones and that female dog pee is worthy of more attention than male dog pee. Wolves leave a scent trail in a similar way, so it's possible dogs are exhibiting an ancestral trait that no longer has much of a useful purpose.

HOW TO TRAIN YOUR HUMAN

You may think you've got your dog fairly well trained, but what about all the things your dog has taught you to do? Open the back door, retrieve a toy from under the sofa, hand out biscuits, throw a ball, go and fetch the ball to throw it again, leave a space free on the bed. The list goes on and on and most dog owners have been trained to do these kinds of things.

We feel pretty pleased with ourselves when we've trained a dog to sit. Dogs soon realise that they get a treat if they sit so they start sitting at our feet in the hope of a reward, even when we haven't asked them to. If you give a dog a treat in this situation, it's actually you who's obeying a command, not your dog. Similarly, if you feed your dog titbits from the table, you are a very well-trained human.

Dogs are extremely adept at manipulating us to their own ends. Like small children, they employ a range of attention-seeking behaviours to get us to focus on their needs. They bark, they nuzzle, they whine, they tilt their heads, they hop from one foot to the other until we break off from what we're doing and pay attention to them.

Researchers have set up experiments to observe how dogs show humans what to do. A researcher places a tasty snack somewhere out of the dog's reach and then watches what the dog does when the owner (who hasn't seen where the treat was placed) enters the room. The dogs tend to look at the desired object and then back at the owner, then gaze in the direction of the object and bark at it.

You don't need to be a scientist to have observed this behaviour – every dog owner has witnessed it. Perhaps this is why the actions of life-saving fictional dogs, such as Lassie, rings true despite being obviously far-fetched. Lassie need only bark a few times and turn her head for someone to understand that she's giving instructions: 'What's that, Lassie? A child's fallen down a well? OK, we'd better organise a rescue party.' Less-dramatic versions of this happen in every dog-owning household every single day – but it's usually because the dog is telling us they want a biscuit or a cuddle or a toy.

CAN DOGS SMELL FEAR?

The idea that dogs know when people are afraid of them is a commonly held piece of folk wisdom, but can it really be true that dogs are that perceptive about human emotion? In order for this to be possible, frightened humans would have to smell differently from calm and collected ones. People do tend to sweat more when they are afraid, but it's not clear if scared sweat actually smells different from, say, gym sweat – although some animals do appear to produce alarm pheromones.

Dogs do have an amazing sense of smell, but they are also keen observers of human behaviour. If they do respond to fearful people it may be because they are experts at reading body language. However they do it, dogs probably do know when people are afraid, but it doesn't necessarily follow that they are more likely to attack a fearful person, as is often believed. Dogs, in fact, are more likely to attack when they themselves are afraid.

DOG'S MIND

What makes our dogs tick

Dogs and humans get on so well together it's easy to believe that we are of one mind. Most dog owners think they know when their pets are happy or sad, lonely or bored. Many of us go further and are absolutely convinced that our canine friends can express a range of complex emotions from jealousy and guilt to embarrassment, disappointment and even grief. We also like to think that our dogs understand us and that our empathetic companions instinctively know when we are feeling miserable and in need of a dog-hug. But what's really going on in a dog's head? How do they make sense of the world and whatever do they think of us?

DOES MY DOG LOVE ME?

Your dog does bum-waggle excitement every time you come home, whimpers in despair when you ask a friend to hold the lead while you go to the loo, and rests a head lovingly on your knee at every possible opportunity. This must be love, surely? Perhaps, but the meaning of love is best left to poets and philosophers – scientists prefer to study what they call attachment, which is easier to measure.

Research has shown that hand-reared wolf cubs do not show the same level of attachment to their owners as puppies reared in the same way. Four-month old cubs and puppies were monitored for how they greeted their owner, their willingness to play with their owner above other people, and how long they stood at the door after their owner had gone. The tests suggest that dogs are much more attached to individual caregivers than wolves. Other research has also shown that dogs choose humans over their littermates.

Something called the Strange Situation test, originally devised to examine mother–child attachment, has also been tried out on dogs. The test involves observing the dog's reaction to being repeatedly separated from and then reunited with their owner as well as their responses to a series of encounters with a stranger. Guess what? The dogs were much happier when their owners were present and greeted them enthusiastically every time they returned.

All this love has some chemistry behind it – namely oxytocin, a hormone produced by mammals (including humans) which is believed to play an important role in bonding, both within and between species. A nasal oxytocin spray has been shown to make dogs more affectionate towards humans and other dogs (trials have also revealed that the hormone promotes affection among humans, too). Most of the time, of course, dogs produce their own natural love juice, which is why we love them back so much.

ARE YOU THINKING WHAT I'M THINKING?

Human beings have the capacity to understand that other people may know things we don't know and not know things we do. If you see your dog pee in a shoe, for example, you know that the person who walks through the door five minutes later and puts their foot in it doesn't know about the pee, even though you do. This ability to comprehend that other people have a mind of their own is called 'theory of mind' and has often been considered to be uniquely human – one of the qualities which separates us from other animals, along with language, tool making and the ability to fake laugh at other people's bad jokes. But some dog behaviour researchers have pondered on the possibility that other animals may also be able to put themselves in the shoes of others. Chimpanzees, perhaps, or maybe even dogs.

In order to explore whether dogs really do have a theory of mind, you need some really good tests. The standard experiment for demonstrating theory of mind in children involves a scenario acted out by puppets. Two puppets are present when an object is placed in a basket. One puppet leaves, and the remaining puppet mischievously moves the object to another basket. The child involved in the test is then asked where the

DOGTIONARY CORNER

Pet, n. /pɛt/ Used to describe a domestic animal since around 1500, 'pet' is a word of Scottish origin which used to refer to a hand-reared farm animal such as a lamb. 'Pet' is also commonly used as a term of endearment in some parts of the UK.

absent puppet will look for the object when they return. Until the age of about four, children don't understand that the puppet doesn't know what they know and young minds expect the puppet to look in the new hiding place. It's only when they're old enough to have acquired a theory of mind that they realise that the puppet can't know the object has moved, and will look in the original location.

Unfortunately, puppetry is wasted on dogs. Not to be deterred, some researchers developed an alternative test to see if a Belgian Shepherd dog called Phillip could demonstrate that he understood the perspective of others. Various objects were hidden in boxes which were then locked and the keys hidden. Phillip was a trained assistance dog, so he knew how to guide people to objects. Sure enough, he seemed to understand that people who had not been present when the key was hidden needed more help finding it than those who had been in the room all along.

This one experiment falls a long way short of proving that dogs do have a theory of mind and subsequent attempts to replicate the experiment have had mixed results. But it's early days in the science of dog cognition and researchers have only recently got the bit between the teeth on this topic. No doubt more will be revealed as more work is done on figuring out how sensitive dogs are to human behaviour, but all we know for certain right now is that we don't know whether our dogs can imagine the world from our point of view or not.

MIRROR, MIRROR ON THE WALL

Dogs don't need mirrors. They don't have to put an outfit together every morning and they don't feel the need to inspect the bags under their eyes. Even so, researchers in behavioural science just love putting a mirror in front of a dog, or any other animal they can lay their hands on.

The mirror self-recognition test was developed in the 1970s as a way of determining whether animals have self-awareness. Most dog owners will have observed their pets looking at themselves in a mirror. Dogs typically react to their own reflection as if it is another dog; they often bark at it or back away. Sometimes they look behind the mirror to find out where this other dog is hiding. In other words, they fail the mirror test. Chimpanzees, by contrast, take a couple of days to understand that the reflection is not, in fact, an intruder and recognise the image as their own. They even use the mirror to look at bits of their bodies they can't normally see (yes, chimpanzees really do stand in front of a mirror looking at their own bums). Other animals to have passed the mirror test include dolphins, elephants and magpies. But not dogs, who, like human children up to about two years of age, can't get to grips with the fact that they're looking at their own reflection.

WHY THE GUILTY FACE?

Rationally, we know that dogs can't possibly understand that running off with a sock is 'bad' or that taking a tennis ball from another dog in the park is unethical, yet we have a very strong instinct to project our views of good and bad behaviour onto our dogs. This is compounded by the fact that dogs do exceptionally good 'guilty' faces. You come home to a puddle of pee, a chewed-up shoe or an overturned rubbish bin and your dog gives you the guiltiest look you've ever seen. So what's going on?

For a start, nobody likes to be stared at and when you've discovered your dog's misdemeanour you probably stare at them – and possibly point and raise your voice. Anyone's natural response to this is to avert your gaze, which is exactly what dogs do. If you're really angry, they might cower a bit as well. Unfortunately for them, this posture coincides with what humans interpret as a guilty look. Their reaction has nothing to do with the widdle on the carpet they had two hours earlier, and everything to do with the look on your face right now.

One researcher has tested this by putting a snack within dog reach and then asking the dog's owner to give a command to leave the food. The owner then leaves the room. When the owners returned, they were told to react as if their dogs had eaten the snack, even when they hadn't. The owners told their dogs off and got a guilty response back – gaze averted, head down, sloping off. This behaviour was clearly not out of guilt – the dogs were entirely innocent – but a reaction to their unhappy owners.

SWEET DREAMS

Dogs often twitch, quiver, kick out, whine and make an array of funny noises while they're asleep. It looks like they're dreaming and, naturally, any devoted owner assumes these dreams are sweet ones of gambolling through woods and chasing squirrels. But given that dogs can't bore us with their dream stories, can we be sure that dogs really do dream?

Well, they exhibit similar signs to dreaming humans – moving, making noises and so on. In particular, dogs (along with most other mammals) go through rapid-eye movement (REM) stages in their sleep. REM is strongly associated with dreaming in humans so it's not too outlandish to assume that dogs also dream during this stage. What they dream about, however, will probably always be a secret.

WHICH ARE THE BRAINIEST BREEDS?

Intelligence is a slippery subject. What is it exactly? Innate abilities or stuff you've learned? How do you assess the intelligence of someone who's a maths genius and compare it with the intelligence of someone who's useless at maths but brilliant at languages? The same problems apply when trying to assess intelligence in dogs. How do you measure a dog that's good at herding against one that's got retrieving skills? How do you factor in the fact the trainability may be affected by things like height or skull shape – giving some dogs an advantage when it comes to seeing human commands? Is it fair to judge a dog that's had lots of training by the same criteria as one who's never been to an obedience class?

Most people have heard that Border Collies and Labradors are highly intelligent whereas Boxers, say, or Afghan Hounds are not quite so sharp. But every dog is an individual, so does it ever make sense to talk about all the dogs belonging to one breed being more or less intelligent than all the members of another breed? What about mongrels? Where do they fit into it all? Most scientists agree that there is as much behavioural variation within breeds as between them so a truly wise human would think twice before deciding whether a dog was stupid or smart merely by breed alone.

CLOCK WATCH DOGS

Does your dog have a clock in his stomach? Does he give you a little nudge every time it gets close to feeding time? That's probably the food-anticipatory circadian rhythms at work. Circadian rhythms are biological processes that roughly follow a daily cycle. They exist in nearly all living things, including plants and microbes. This complex branch of biology explains why daisies open in the morning and rabbits retire at dusk. They are also the reason your dog knows when you should get out of bed and when you should get busy with the tin opener.

WHAT TIME DO YOU CALL THIS?

Does your dog know when you're coming home? You might think they do, but the truth is they probably don't. The reason this belief persists may be down to confirmation bias – how we notice things that confirm our hunches while ignoring things that cast doubt on them. So, you notice your dog looking out the window and conclude your home-coming was anticipated. In fact, your dog may have looked out the window many times that day – but you didn't come home every time.

A MATTER OF BREEDING

Encounters with mutts and pedigrees

Most of the dogs that have ever existed have made their own decisions about who is a promising mate, and this is still the case today for many of the millions of free-ranging dogs that live around the world. But alongside this free love, there is a long history of human interference in canine reproduction. People have been selectively breeding dogs for thousands of years in an attempt to produce the perfect hunter, herder, guard dog or lap-sized companion and the result is the extraordinary variety of dogs that can be seen in any park on any day. Yet the notion that each different breed is unique and should be kept that way has only been around for the past 150 years or so. Pedigree dogs with pure bloodlines going way back to the Roman Empire, the Ming Dynasty or the age of the Knights Templar are the stuff of fancy rather than science. The fact is that even the proudest pedigree dog almost certainly has a long line of mutts somewhere in their family tree.

WHAT EXACTLY IS A PEDIGREE DOG?

Put simply, a pedigree dog is one which belongs to a recognised breed. A pedigree may be registered with a national or international kennel club organisation and have documentation detailing a pedigree going back several generations.

In theory, pedigree dogs belonging to the same breed should be more or less uniform in appearance (and it is mainly physical characteristics that are up for consideration in the pedigree show ring). In practice, of course, variations inevitably occur, which is why even the most carefully bred pedigree may never have a shot at Best in Show.

There also a number of registers for working pedigree dogs, such as the one kept by the International Sheepdog Society and the Masters of Foxhounds Association stud book. All of these meticulously kept records of sires (fathers) and dams (mothers) are supposed to ensure the purity of the breeds in question. Yet, despite this attention to genetic detail, breeds are not fixed. They change over time and there isn't always agreement on what the breed standard should be in the first place. The Germans, for instance, recognise nine different varieties of Dachshunds, whereas there are only six in the UK. If you breed a standard Dachshund with a miniature one, it's still a Dachshund, but is it still a pedigree? In the loosest sense, yes – but you wouldn't be able to get a fancy certificate listing the names of all its great grandparents.

DOGTIONARY CORNER

Bitch, v. /bɪtʃ/ Despite that fact that female dogs never gossip behind each other's backs, the verb 'to bitch' has come to mean spiteful talk directed at or about others.

THE SHIFTING WORLD
OF RECOGNISED BREEDS

Anyone who's ever popped into the British Museum knows that dogs came in different shapes and sizes way back in history. Pottery, mosaics, paintings, carvings and various other artefacts from the ancient civilisations of Egypt, Greece, Rome, China and the Near East reveal that a range of canines has existed for at least 4000 years. Among the oldest of these is a dog which looks very like a modern sight hound, such as a Greyhound or Saluki. But let's not get carried away. Just because the Egyptians had lean, long-legged hunting hounds doesn't mean that that the sight hounds of today are the direct descendents of the pharaoh's pets.

For most of human history, where dogs have been selectively bred they have been chosen primarily for function. Crosses between different types of dogs, both accidental and on purpose, would have been commonplace and there is no evidence in any breed of an unbroken line of descent back to any point much before the Victorian period.

Foxhounds were ahead of the pack and have had their family trees recorded since as early as 1717 (pedigree racehorses didn't get a register until 1791). But the idea that dogs could and should be categorised according to some apparently logical set of criteria didn't become widespread until the mania for naming, classifying and ordering the entire natural world into distinct and separate groups took hold in the mid-19th century.

The first ever conformation dog show in the UK took place in Newcastle in 1859. Only two types of dogs were listed; Pointers and Setters. The first monthly register of dogs was published by the Kennel Club in 1880; 43 breeds were listed. Since then, the number of breeds recognised by canine organisations around the world has mushroomed to over 350.

DNA analysis reveals that there is often as much divergence within as between breeds, indicating that the ancestors of even long-established breeds were genetically diverse. So, in many cases, a breed exists more in the eye of the beholder than in any significant biological differences.

IS YOUR ST BERNARD BENEVOLENT?
DOES YOUR IRISH WATER SPANIEL
HAVE A SENSE OF HUMOUR?

According to official breed standards the Pointer is kind, the Shih Tzu is independent, the Afghan Hound is dignified and the Italian Greyhound may appear aloof. This is a bit like saying the French are chic or the Italians are passionate. There may be a grain of truth in it somewhere, but it's still a massively sweeping generalisation. Dogs are individuals, just as people are. You get affectionate Basset Hounds, as the breed standard suggests, but also ones that are not so fussed. Boxers can be self-assured, as advertised, but you might still get one that's a bit insecure. A dog's personality is much more strongly determined by their upbringing and life experience than by their breed.

That said, there clearly are some heritable differences between breeds. Collies will herd, for instance, even if they've never been near a sheep farm. Labradors will carry objects very gently in their mouths, Beagles fixate on a scent trail and Whippets run like the clappers. Still, these are very specific behaviours and it's much harder to pin more general character traits to individual breeds. Personality is a complex combination of genetics and experience and dogs of any breed can be friendly or aggressive, placid or alert.

Interestingly, comparative studies on dog breeds show that the evidence points to a much larger difference if you survey dog owners than if you carry out controlled experiments. In other words, there is little objective evidence that breed significantly influences character, but there is a lot of anecdotal evidence. This could be because scientists still need to do some work in this area, or it could be down to the fact that dog owners see what they expect to see.

There's an element of 'give a dog a bad (or good) name' at work here – our behaviour towards dogs of different types may be influenced by our preconceptions about their supposed breed characteristics – which could, in turn, affect how they actually behave. If you're told a certain breed is affectionate, for example, you might act accordingly – creating a dog that learns to love cuddles. If, on the other hand, you've been led to believe your breed is independent and aloof, you may be less inclined to lavish the love.

The extent to which breed characteristics are fact or fantasy is open to debate, but there's no doubt that our feelings about different dog breeds are at least partly shaped by our personal experience with dogs and may also be influenced by the media. Dogs are just as much the victims of stereotypes as people are.

A CLASS OF THEIR OWN

The Kennel Club recognises seven dog groups: Gundog; Hound; Pastoral; Terrier; Toy; Utility; Working. At first glance, it looks like grouping dogs together with like-minded canines is a purely practical affair – put dogs together with other dogs who do (or did) similar jobs. But separating the sheep from the goat herders (so to speak) is not a precise science.

Does a Yorkshire Terrier, for instance, have more in common with a Pug than it does with an Australian Terrier? The Kennel Club seems to think so, which is why the Yorkie is in the Toy group, alongside Pugs, whereas the Australian Terrier is grouped with the other Terriers. To further illustrate the sometimes random nature of canine classification, take the example of the Spanish Water Dog, the Portuguese Water Dog and the Standard Poodle. They are all in different groups (gundog, working and utility, respectively) even though they share a similar look and were all originally used for the same purpose (retrieving game from water).

Classifying different types of dogs into distinct groups is no easy task, but people have been having a go at it for a surprisingly long time. The Roman naturalist, Pliny the Elder, divided dogs into six different categories: house or guardian dogs; shepherd dogs; sporting dogs; war dogs; scent hounds; and sight hounds. Much later, Dr Caius (who was physician to Queen Elizabeth I) wrote a book about dogs which used three categories to reflect the role and status of dogs in human society: generous (in other words, dogs used in hunting or as companions); rustic (dogs that worked on farms such as sheepdogs and guard dogs) and degenerate (a rather unkind expression, to our ears, for every other type of dog).

Of course, most dogs these days (in the Western world, at least) are primarily companions, so we could do away with these artificial distinctions and just call them all friends.

The Ten Groups Recognised by the World Canine Organisation

The Fédération Cynologique Internationale is the world canine organisation and recognises more distinct breeds than any other body. Nearly 350 breeds from around the globe are divided into the following ten groups.

1. Sheepdogs and Cattledogs (except Swiss Cattledogs)

2. Terriers

3. Spitz and primitive types

4. Pointing dogs

5. Companion and Toy dogs

6. Pinscher and Schnauzer – Molossoid and Swiss Mountain and Cattledogs

7. Dachshunds

8. Scenthounds and related breeds

9. Retrievers – flushing dogs – water dogs

10. Sighthounds

A MATTER OF BREEDING

THE DESCENT OF DOG – DARWIN'S CANINE MUSES

Even the great naturalist, Charles Darwin, was flummoxed by the sheer variety he observed in the domestic dog.

Darwin was a lifelong dog owner who had dogs of all shapes and sizes, including Bob the retriever, Bran the Deerhound and a terrier called Polly, who was used as an example in one of Darwin's books; *The Expression of the Emotions in Man and Animals*. His observations of his own much-loved pets certainly provided plenty of food for thought.

Darwin came to his theory of evolution through natural selection partly through observing the effects of artificial selection in domestic animals. He also made copious notes about his own dogs' behaviour and pondered on issues such as whether dogs could experience jealousy or express kindness. Darwin referred to his dogs frequently in his notes, letters and published works, so it's not too farfetched to say that dogs played a significant part in one of the most important scientific breakthroughs of the modern age.

TEN BREEDS THAT SOMEONE MADE UP

Some breeds come about because of a naturally occurring variation which someone decides is appealing enough to warrant reproduction. Short legs, for example, probably just happened naturally, but were then perpetuated by someone who saw potential in a Basset Hound or a Dachshund. Other changes may occur as unintended consequences of selecting for something else completely different – genetics are unpredictable. But that doesn't stop some determined aficionados from trying to create the dog of their dreams. Over the page are ten breeds that exist because someone really, really wanted them to.

1. **Jack Russell Terrier:** Reverend John
   Russell (known as 'the sporting parson'
   because of his love of hunting) acquired
   a Fox Terrier-type dog in the early 19th
   century and set about establishing a line of
   terriers that had enough stamina to follow
   horses while being small enough to go to

   ground after prey. They were named after him some time after his
   death and have been immensely popular ever since.

2. **Cavalier King Charles Spaniel:** The toy spaniels favoured by both
   Charles I and II were immortalised by Sir Edwin Landseer in his
   1845 painting *The Cavalier's Pets*. But when American dog enthusiast,
   Roswell Eldridge, visited England in the 1920s he was disappointed
   to find that the King Charles Spaniel no longer looked like the
   Landseer version and had acquired a shorter snout.
   Determined to put things right, he offered
   a £25 prize for five years running to be
   awarded to the best 'long-faced spaniels
   of the old type'. The result was a new
   dog that looked like the old one and was
   eventually recognised as a separate breed.

3. **Cesky Terrier:** Czech dog owner and geneticist Dr Frantisek Horak
   enjoyed hunting with his Scottish Terriers and also took a shine to
   Sealyham Terriers. He wasn't entirely satisfied with either breed,
   though, and thought that a dog with the qualities of both would suit
   him better. He began crossing his two preferred breeds in the 1930s,
   but it wasn't until after the Second
   World War that the project really got
   off the ground. In only six generations,
   he had created the dogs which are the
   ancestors of all the Cesky Terriers in
   the world today.

4. **Sealyham Terrier:** John
Edwardes, a retired army captain,
developed the Sealyham Terrier
in the late 19th century to work
alongside his Otter Hounds
on the Sealyham estate in
Pembrokeshire, west Wales. He
wanted the perfect working terrier that could multitask – working
in burrows, over ground and in water. Edwardes didn't keep any
records of his breeding programme and there is much speculation
about which breeds went into the mix. The Dandie Dinmont, West
Highland Terrier and Pembroke Corgi have all been suggested as
possibilities.

5. **Dobermann:** Louis Dobermann was a German tax collector who
also worked as the local dog catcher. Naturally, his clients weren't
always pleased to see him so, sometime around the 1870s, he began
developing a dog that would give him some protection. He had his
pick of the dog pound to choose from, but it's not clear exactly which
dogs were
used in the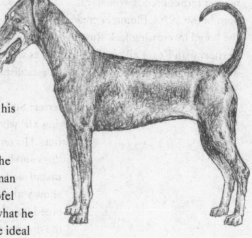
foundation
of his breed.
Dobermanns
were named
after their
creator shortly after his
death in 1894.

6. **Eurasier:** During the
1940s and 50s, German
professor Julius Wipfel
set out to produce what he
considered to be the ideal

Spitz-type dog. He was influenced by the work of the Nobel Prize-winning naturalist, Konrad Lorenz, and believed the Spitz could be improved by combining European and Asian bloodlines. The breed's name reflects this mixed heritage. Wipfel began by crossing the German Wolfspitz with the Chow Chow, later he introduced Samoyeds as well. The Eurasier was recognised by the German Kennel Club in 1973.

7. **Plummer Terrier:** Brian Plummer was a leading light in the world of working terriers until his death in 2003. He attempted to revive a couple of extinct breeds and his name is now attached to one of the newest terrier breeds, which was born in the 1970s. Plummer created the breed by crossing Jack Russell

Terriers with Fox, Fell and Bull terriers as well as a dose of Beagle. The Plummer Terrier Association was established in the mid-1990s.

8. **Lucas Terrier:** Sir Jocelyn Lucas was a long-serving MP who also bred Sealyham Terriers. His terriers were working dogs and he gradually became dissatisfied with the way the show variety of his favoured breed was being changed, making the dog unsuitable for going to

ground. In the 1940s he began
creating his own ideal terrier
by crossing Sealyhams with
Norfolk Terriers. So pleased
was he with the result that he
called the new terrier after
himself.

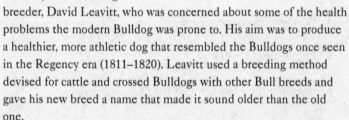

9. **Olde English Bulldogge:**
   This new version of an old
   breed was created in the
   1970s by American dog
   breeder, David Leavitt, who was concerned about some of the health
   problems the modern Bulldog was prone to. His aim was to produce
   a healthier, more athletic dog that resembled the Bulldogs once seen
   in the Regency era (1811–1820). Leavitt used a breeding method
   devised for cattle and crossed Bulldogs with other Bull breeds and
   gave his new breed a name that made it sound older than the old
   one.

10. **Labradoodle:** This cross-breed was initially developed in the 1980s
    by Australian dog breeder, Wally Conron, for a very specific purpose.
    The Australian Guide Dog Association was looking for a dog suitable
    for a visually impaired person with allergies. The idea was that a
    Labrador's trustworthy, trainable qualities
    combined with a Poodle's
    non-shedding coat would
    produce the ideal assistance
    dog. Little did Conron
    know that his creation
    would become so popular
    that dozens of other Poodle
    crosses would follow in its
    wake.

Ten novelty names for newly minted cross-breeds

1. *Cockerpoo*: Cocker Spaniel × Poodle

2. *Schnoodle*: Schnauzer × Poodle

3. *Aussiedoodle*: Australian Shepherd × Poodle

4. *Pekapoo*: Pekingese × Poodle

5. *Puggle*: Beagle × Pug

6. *Beagalier*: Beagle × Cavalier King Charles Spaniel

7. *Jackhuahua*: Jack Russell × Chihuahua

8. *Bostie*: Boston Terrier × White Highland Terrier

9. *Gollie*: Golden Retriever × Border Collie

10. *Saint Dane*: Great Dane × St Bernard

EVERY DOG HAS ITS DAY

A look back at some dog
breeds of the past

There are all sorts of occupations that have long since faded into history as technology has moved on and lifestyles have changed. Who needs a reeve, a mudlark or a coachman these days? The same thing has happened to jobs for dogs. New inventions replaced canine labourers and changing attitudes to animal welfare put some dogs out of work. Dog carts, once a familiar sight around London's Smithfield Market, were made illegal in the 19th century and the horribly cruel 'sport' of baiting animals with dogs was banned in 1835. Many dog breeds survived redundancy and became the companions we still have today, but some types of dogs failed to make the transition to domesticity and are now no more than a memory.

ROUND AND ROUND WE GO

Many working dogs just can't wait to get to the office. Anyone who's seen a sheepdog herd a flock or watched a food-detection Beagle sniff a suitcase knows what job satisfaction looks like. But one of the saddest sights in canine history must be a Turnspit at work. These unhappy little dogs performed the task their name suggests; turning a spit of meat over a roasting fire. The breed was first mentioned in print in 1576 and they continued to work in pockets of Britain until well into the 19th century.

The traditional British joint of beef was originally roasted over an open fire, rather than in an oven. This took at least four hours and involved constant turning to prevent parts of the meat becoming burnt. In the middle ages, this task was given to a servant (the original turnspits), but at some point in the Tudor period someone had the bright idea of getting a dog to turn the wheel instead. A contraption resembling a giant hamster wheel was attached to the wall by the fireplace and connected to the turning spit above the fire. The dogs used were small with long bodies and short legs and they were often kept in pairs and worked in shifts. They had to trot round the wheel in the heat and smoke of the fire for hours on end and were no doubt ill-treated by kitchen staff if they dared stop to catch their breath.

The invention of clock jacks (a clockwork mechanism driven by weights) in the 16th century provided an alternative to the Turnspit dog, but they were expensive and initially only available to the wealthy. This new technology gradually came down in price, but dog wheels continued to be prevalent in homes and inns, particularly across the West Country and Wales, during the 17th and 18th centuries and a handful of Turnspits were still working until around 1850.

There are a number of pubs and museums in Britain where you can still see dog wheels (happily, without a dog actually working in them) or, better still, you can see a real Turnspit (albeit stuffed) in the Abergavenny Museum in Wales. Whiskey, as the little dog is known, looks something like a cross between a Dachshund and a squirrel and is thought to be the only surviving example of a Turnspit in Britain. Whiskey was given to the museum in 1959, although it's not clear exactly when the dog was in employment. Turnspits were more or less extinct by 1900, which was a bit too early for them to have been taken up by the emerging hobby of dog breeding and showing. Their lowly status and odd appearance may also explain why they didn't appeal to the dog fancy set. If only they'd found a

Victorian champion Turnspits might have survived to this day and become non-working companions, sitting on our sofas and expecting us to prepare their food.

DOGTIONARY CORNER

Cur, n. /kɜː(r)/ Now usually an insult which suggests a dog of little worth, the word 'cur' was originally just another word for dog. The word appears in a number of Shakespeare's plays as an insult for people.

CARTING DOGS

Horses and donkeys did a lot of the pulling, towing, hauling and carting work in the era before the motor vehicle but there was a time when dogs, too, pulled carts for their keep. In the 19th century, carts pulled by dogs delivered meat and fruit and vegetables from London markets. Two or more large dogs would be harnessed to a towing shaft at the front of the cart. They were often supervised by young boys, who would walk alongside the cart or sit in it as if driving a horse and carriage. Dog carts were also used to transport children and dog cart races were common. It was generally a harsh life for the dogs and the practice drew the attention of early animal welfare campaigners and was eventually outlawed in Britain. In Belgium and Holland, however, draught dogs were still a common sight into the 20th century, where they were often used to deliver milk. Visitors to the Lowlands were clearly struck by this quaint transportation and dog carts were often depicted on postcards.

ONE DOG, MANY PUBS

The Talbot was a white hound which is no longer with us but whose name and image lives on in the name and signs of dozens of British pubs. Possibly the ancestor of today's Bloodhound, the Talbot may have come to Britain along with the Normans in the 11th century and is associated with families of noble lineage. The Talbot features in the heraldic crests of a number of English families, notably the Talbot family of Shrewsbury. In heraldry, the Talbot represents the qualities of courage, vigilance and loyalty. In pubs, it represents a nice old pub that's probably quite cosy and has a selection of real ales. The same may be true of the Fox and Hounds or the Greyhound Inn, but the Talbot is the only extinct dog you'll find on a pub sign.

Ten British breeds whose days may be numbered

If you're looking for a dog these days you're really spoilt for choice. Breeds you'd never heard of a decade or so ago are now readily available and dogs that were once only known within their home region have now gone global. On top of that, cross-breeds have become immensely popular and, best of all, many more people are choosing to adopt rescue dogs of mixed or unknown parentage. Contemporary trends in canine choices could be leaving some of our older breeds behind and some British dogs are but a yelp away from extinction. Breeds are considered vulnerable if there are fewer than 300 puppy registrations a year. Some of the dogs on the endangered list have never been very commonplace, but there are some household names who are dangerously close to becoming history. These ten British breeds had fewer than 200 Kennel Club puppy registrations in 2013:

1. Bloodhound

2. Collie (smooth)

3. Dandie Dinmont Terrier

4. Smooth Fox Terrier

5. Lancashire Heeler

6. Manchester Terrier

7. Skye Terrier

8. Cardigan Welsh Corgi

9. Otterhound

10. Curly Coated Retriever

TUMBLING AROUND

We don't know much about the dog that was described in the 16th century as a Tumbler, but it seems they used a kind of decoy technique to catch rabbits and were probably similar to a small Greyhound or Lurcher. A book called *Of Englishe Dogges*, which was published in 1576, describes the Tumbler as a dog 'which compasseth all by craftes, fraudes, subtelties and deceiptes.' In other words, instead of attacking rabbits head on, the Tumbler would prance around playfully, jumping and tumbling and generally messing about until the rabbits were lulled into a false sense of security. Then, all of a sudden, the Tumbler would pounce on their prey. This unusual hunting method probably disappeared as guns became more reliable and readily available.

ONE OBSOLETE DOG JOB

These days there are all manner of jobs with dogs: grooming, training, doggy day care or even dog hydrotherapy or acupuncture. But one dog-related profession is thankfully now obsolete. For about 300 hundred years, churches around Europe employed someone called a dog whipper. The tools of their trade were a long whip and a pair of dog tongs and their objective was to make dogs behave in church, or to stay out altogether.

In the days before 'no dogs' signs existed, it was regarded as normal for people to arrive at church with their dogs in tow, some churches even provided a special pew for the dogs of the well-to-do. Some dogs set up home inside churches, which wasn't much of a problem most of the week, but irked some clergymen on Sundays.

This is where the dog whipper came in. He was employed to restore order should bouts of barking or fighting break out. One of the last recorded dog whippers was employed by Exeter Cathedral in 1856 and there is still a room there known as the dog whipper's flat.

HERD INSTINCT

———◆———

The story of a pastoral partnership

Wolves are predators by nature and our dogs share their instinct to hunt, yet one of the ways they've made themselves most useful to humans throughout history is by helping to look after livestock. Dogs have shepherded flocks away from cliff edges, sought out lambs lost in snowdrifts, made sure cattle stuck to the path and protected all kinds of farm animals from predators – including their very own ancestor, the wolf. Humans have harnessed the natural instincts of dogs and bred and trained them to be helpmates rather than competitors. This partnership has been vital to sheep and cattle farmers for many hundreds of years and herding dogs are still performing this essential function in many parts of the world today.

SHEPHERD'S BEST FRIEND

It's hard to overestimate the importance of a good dog to a shepherd. Even in this era of advanced technology, nothing is quite as effective as a dog for keeping a flock under control (although they often work alongside quad bikes these days). This partnership began in ancient times when humans began farming sheep, which were the second species after dogs to be fully domesticated. The two main functions of the shepherd's dog are guarding, which often suits a large, muscular dog, and herding, which calls for a more agile, quick-witted canine.

There are dozens of types of livestock guarding and herding dogs, but one definitely stands out from the crowd. The dog we know today as the Border Collie (the name of the officially recognised show variety) or the working sheep dog (the term preferred by participants in sheep trial events) is believed by many to be the most talented herding dog that's ever existed. Originally from the Scottish borders, this nimble sheep dog was developed over many generations of careful breeding and training.

Curiously enough, the working sheep dog actually uses some of the same tactics as wolves to round up the flock. Wolves hunt as a team, with one or several pack members circling the prey and herding it towards a spot where it can more easily be killed. Working sheep dogs do a similar thing, but stop before the killing part. The dog works in close partnership with the shepherd and responds to a series of spoken commands as well as whistles. The shepherd's best friend crouches and creeps and stalks with all the concentration of a true professional and fixes the sheep with an intense stare, a characteristic Collie technique known as 'strong eye'.

Collie-type dogs have been used to herd sheep, ducks, turkeys, reindeer and even ostriches. These highly trainable dogs are certainly high achievers, but one thing the breed is not always so good at is settling down to a quiet life as a family pet. The working instincts are strong and this is one dog that definitely needs a job or a hobby.

LOOKING SHEEPISH

Two Hungarian herding breeds really go the extra distance to fit in with the flock. Both the Komondor and the Puli have distinctive thick, curly coats that form cords similar to dreadlocks. This weatherproof coat provides protection in case of attack by predators and is also a cunning form of disguise. These mop-topped canines blend in with the sheep and could cause an unsuspecting predator quite a shock. Both breeds are rare and most easily seen at dog shows, although there are still some working with sheep in Hungary and a few are working as guard dogs in the United States.

PASTURES NEW

Humans have been moving their livestock from upland pastures in summer to lower grazing areas in winter for thousands of years. This seasonal movement is called transhumance and often relies on livestock guarding dogs to get sheep and cattle up and down mountains as well as protect them from predators. There are dozens of breeds of dog with a livestock guarding heritage, such as the Maremma Sheepdog from Italy and the Estrela Mountain Dog from Portugal.

This range of breeds probably didn't initially come about because of direct and methodical intervention by humans; selective breeding wasn't commonplace until towards the end of the 19th century and livestock guardians have been with us since the earliest days of farming. It's thought that what actually happened was a more haphazard series of adaptations to local conditions coupled with human preferences which favoured some types of dog while disadvantaging others.

Dogs with the physical characteristics necessary to survive the climate, for example, were more likely to live long enough to reproduce. Not surprisingly, many of these breeds have thick coats and tend to be fairly large and muscular. People also played their part in shaping these breeds, but not so much by actively selecting which dogs to breed. Rather, dogs that had desirable traits were more likely to have been given food and access to shelter, which would have boosted their chances of passing on those traits. Dogs with undesirable characteristics, by contrast, would have been culled or neglected. Dogs that displayed aggression towards livestock would not have been tolerated – to put it bluntly, they were often killed – so that particular characteristic would not have been passed on to future generations.

HERDING TO PROTECT PREDATORS

It's not only livestock that can be protected by herding dogs – in one pioneering scheme, predators also benefit from having a livestock guardian about. A conservation project in Namibia came up with an inspired way to protect cheetahs. Given that one of the main threats to cheetahs comes from farmers who see them as a threat to their sheep and goats, a programme was established to protect livestock from cheetahs in order to protect cheetahs from farmers. The secret weapon in this effective conservation strategy is the Anatolian Shepherd Dog, a breed which was developed as a livestock guardian in its native Turkey. Evidence suggests that the introduction of these dogs reduces predation rates by at least 80% and has made local farmers much more tolerant of cheetahs and other endangered predators.

DOGTIONARY CORNER

Dog, v. /dɒg/ Used as a verb, the word 'dog' means to follow persistently (and possibly annoyingly). This usage has been around since the early 16th century.

THIS LITTLE DOGGY WENT TO MARKET

Persuading cattle to walk from farm to market is no small challenge, but you can't fit many cows in a horse-driven cart so farmers had to walk with their livestock until the locomotive engine was invented. There are records from as early as the 13th century of Welsh cattle being taken by road to the market town of Gloucester and the trade in cattle along drovers' roads increased throughout the medieval period. Some of the longest journeys involved getting several hundred cattle from the Scottish Highlands all the way to London. Sheep, pigs, turkeys and geese were also taken on these routes to fairs and markets across the country.

Keeping control of hundreds of animals on these long journeys can't have been an easy task, so the drovers depended on dogs to help keep their stock in line as well as to provide protection against thieves. Many of these dogs would have been large sheepdogs, something like a Bearded Collie, an Old English Sheepdog or a now extinct breed, known as the Smithfield Collie (after London's famous meat market). Another useful member of the droving team was the heeler – small dogs such as Corgis, who nipped the ankles of the cattle to get them to move along.

Once the cattle had been safely delivered to market, the drovers would return home by coach with their pockets bulging with money. The drovers' dog were not always afforded such luxury and were expected to find their own way home – a feat not beyond a clever dog covering short distances on familiar routes, but legend has it that some dogs even made their own way back to Scotland from London. It has to be said, however, that it's impossible to know how much of this was actually true and how much was down to a tale spun over a pint of ale in the Drovers' Inn.

The opening of the railways in the 1840s quickly put an end to this centuries-old tradition. The dogs went back to the farms and the once great cattle droves passed into memory. All that is left are some of the original routes, which are still used as roads today, and a whole lot of pubs called the Drovers' Arms.

Ten pastoral breeds you don't see everyday

1. *Smooth Collie*: This short-coated version of the much better known Rough Collie (made famous by the Lassie films) is a Scottish breed that is now very rare.

2. *Australian Cattle Dog*: This tough little dog is the result of crossing a number of different breeds for stamina and agility to produce a dog with the courage and speed to work cattle.

3. *Lancashire Heeler*: This short, hardy cattle dog once had a similar job to the Corgi, working alongside drovers and nipping at the ankles to keep the cattle under control.

4. *Maremma Sheepdog*: This thick-coated, white herding dog comes from the Maremma region of central Italy, where it is very much a working breed.

5. *Kangal Dog*: This large mountain dog is used to guard flocks in the Anatolian plains of its native Turkey and protects them from large predators, including wolves.

6. *Tibetan Mastiff*: This sturdy breed originally guarded livestock, including yak, in the mountains of Himalaya and has also given protection to isolated villages and monasteries.

7. *Icelandic Sheepdog*: This herding dog may have been taken to Iceland by early Scandinavian settlers and has been used to herd horses as well as sheep and other livestock.

8. *Finnish Lapphund*: This is one of a number of similar Nordic breeds which traditionally herded reindeer with the nomadic Sami people of Lapland.

9. *Hungarian Kuvasz*: This flock guardian is reputed to have once been guard dog to royalty and is one of the best-known dogs in Hungary.

10. *Catahoula Leopard Dog*: This herding and hunting dog from Louisiana has been used to hunt all sorts of animals, from raccoons to bears, but they are useful herders as well and sometimes herd pigs.

ON HER MAJESTY'S SERVICE

You might expect a monarch to keep grand, dignified-looking dogs of noble bearing and long ancestry. Instead, however, Queen Elizabeth II opted for Pembroke Corgis. For all their charms, Corgis are never likely to be described as aristocratic, yet this once-humble cattle dog has achieved worldwide renown thanks to a long-standing association with Her Majesty. A Corgi (called Dookie) first joined the Queen's family in 1933, when she was seven years old. She has remained loyal to the breed ever since and has owned over 30 during her reign.

HAIR OF THE DOG

Sheep, goats, rabbits, llamas, yaks. These are the type of animals you expect to provide us with wool – but hair of the dog can also be woven into yarn. In recent years, a bit of a cult hobby has developed around knitting with dog fur. Some enthusiasts have even come up with a name for this unusual wool – chiengora (a mix of the French word for dog – *chien* – with 'angora', a soft rabbit wool). With enough combing and spinning (not to mention patience), it is indeed possible to knit yourself a jumper out of your own dog's hair.

A DOG IN SHEEP'S CLOTHING

Tales of the Salish Wool Dog have been handed down the generations by the Coast Salish – an indigenous American people who live on the Pacific Northwest coast. The existence of a dog kept and selectively bred for its wool was also corroborated in anecdotal accounts by 18th-century European travellers who described how the dogs were shorn once a year, like sheep. Hard evidence, however, has been thin on the ground and it's only very recently that research has confirmed that there may be more to the wool dog story than folklore or travellers' tall tales.

A few years ago, researchers used new techniques to analyse the fibres of blankets woven by the Coast Salish in the 19th century and discovered that they did indeed contain dog hair. It was mixed with the hair of mountain goats, which was highly valued but not readily available. Not only that, the dog fur found in the blankets matched the coat-type of a woolly-haired dog called Mutton, who had belonged to a 19th century ethnographer. For some reason, the dog's pelt had ended up in a drawer in a Washington museum, where it had languished for many a year until being rediscovered in 2004.

Could it be that Mutton was a Salish Wool Dog adopted from the tribes that his owner was studying? Sadly, we may never find out much more about this dog's history. Many indigenous traditions were lost with the arrival of European settlers, who also brought sheep with them. It seems that the practice of keeping dogs for wool had come to an end sometime around 1900 and all that remains are some very unusual blankets.

GAME, SET
AND FETCH

The world of game birds and gundogs

Spaniels, pointers, setters, retrievers and water dogs are collectively classified as gundogs. In fact, though, dogs were pointing at hares, staring out partridges and pulling dead mallards out of ponds long before firearms existed. In these early days, catching game was much more about getting something to eat than sport, but that gradually changed. With the introduction of shotguns in the 18th century, shooting was well on its way to being a respectable, gentlemanly pursuit. Back then the making of a gentleman was the gundog at his side – without this loyal companion many a pheasant (both alive and dead) would never have been found.

WHAT EXACTLY DO GUNDOGS DO?

There are some pretty smart gundogs out there but not one of them can actually pull a trigger, so what exactly is their contribution to the shooting party? Firstly, they have to find the bird (a task most gundogs approach with a great deal of enthusiasm). Then they have to tell their human where it is. Pointers actually do point – albeit using their nose, body, tail and raised front leg rather than an index finger. They stand stock still in this position until the hunter is ready with the gun. Setters also freeze in front of the bird (an action called setting) so it can be located by the hunter. Spaniels use a more boisterous technique called flushing or springing (hence Springer Spaniel), which startles the birds in the direction of the guns.

Finally (and this is the really important bit) they have to go and find the dead bird and then hand it over. Lots of dogs will gladly pick up a dead bird, but getting them to carry it gently in their mouths without causing even a single tooth mark is a lot to ask of a carnivore. That's why a good retriever needs to be bred and trained to have something called a 'soft mouth', which means they can bring the bird back completely undamaged.

Traditional British breeds tend to be specialists; some of them point, others retrieve, so you might need quite a number of dogs on a shoot. Gundogs from mainland Europe, however, tend to be a bit more multi-purpose. The Hungarian Vizsla and the German Pointer, for example, are known as hunt-point-retrieve dogs, or HPR for short. This streamlines the whole process somewhat, and means you can go out for a day's shooting with only one or two dogs.

Of course, the vast majority of people who have gundog breeds don't ever go shooting and many of us prefer feeding ducks to shooting them. Luckily, the skills acquired for the field are readily transferable. Responsive and intelligent, these dogs make rewarding pets for active people and they have taken on new careers as detection dogs, assistance dogs and police dogs.

THE LABRADOR – THE MOST POPULAR DOG ON THE PLANET

The Labrador Retriever has been far and away the most popular breed of dog in the UK for at least two decades, with at least 35,000 puppy registrations a year. Labs (black, yellow and chocolate varieties) are among the most popular breeds in many other countries as well, making it safe to say that the Labrador Retriever is probably the world's favourite canine.

But how did this affable character achieve such a following? Well, it's been a bit of a long journey. Officially, the Labrador is a British dog, although its name would suggest otherwise. But then it's not from Labrador either, but from the neighbouring island of Newfoundland. The Lab isn't even really a gundog, at least not originally. The Labrador's ancestors worked alongside Canadian fishermen and they would pull fishing nets into shore from the chilly North Atlantic Ocean.

The first Labradors arrived in Britain in the late 19th century, but they didn't become widely known until the early years of the 20th. Since then, they've been unstoppable. First they became immensely popular with the shooting set (and made many of the older gundog breeds redundant), then they took on the show world, winning Best in Show at Crufts three times in the 1930s, then they took up positions as guide dogs for the blind (again, eclipsing all other breeds) and now they do all kinds of assistance and detection work. They are also very popular family pets.

Labradors are known to be affectionate, friendly and biddable; character traits that go some way to explain the breed's enduring popularity. On the other hand, they can be over-exuberant and have a reputation for being very destructive in adolescence. They also have a tendency to jump into water at every possible opportunity. Still, the risk of being knocked over by a soaking wet dog or coming home to a room full of sofa stuffing clearly isn't enough to stop people falling for the lovable Lab.

Ten dogs who love getting stuff out of water

1. *Portuguese Water Dog*: This able seadog once retrieved items that had fallen overboard as well as shepherding fish towards nets for Portuguese fishermen. Barack Obama and his family have a Portuguese Water Dog called Bo.

2. *Spanish Water Dog*: Originally used to herd sheep in southern Spain, this versatile dog has also worked in Spanish ports towing boats to shore.

3. *Standard Poodle*: Now largely associated with glamour and hairdressing, this active dog actually started out as a water retriever.

4. *Newfoundland*: This Canadian giant was originally used to trawl fishing nets and has since been credited with saving a number of people from drowning.

5. *Otterhound*: This endangered breed with a thick, weatherproof coat was used to hunt otter in rivers until the 1970s. This now rare breed is an excellent swimmer with webbed feet.

6. *Curly Coated Retriever*: This unusual British breed with short, tight curls was originally bred to hunt waterfowl and is now very rare.

7. *Chesapeake Bay Retriever*: This breed from Maryland came about when two Newfoundland-type pups were rescued from a sinking ship and were later bred with other retriever breeds.

8. *Irish Water Spaniel*: The origins of this oily-coated, waterproof dog are uncertain, but it's at home in the bogs and rivers of Ireland.

9. *Wetterhoun*: The name of this little-known Frisian breed means 'water dog' in Dutch and the dog was used to control otters as well as hunt waterfowl. The breed still sometimes works as a land and water retriever in the Netherlands.

10. *Lagotto Romangolo*: This dog takes its name from the Italian word for 'lake' and has been trained to find truffles, as well as to retrieve from water.

THE FORGOTTEN HISTORY
OF DUCK DECOY DOGS

To most of us, a duck decoy is a replica duck made of wood or plastic that hunters may use to attract real ducks and that some of us may put on the garden pond just to amuse ourselves. But there was once another type of duck decoy which involved constructing an elaborate system of pools, ditches and tunnels in order to supply wildfowl for the table.

There were around 200 of these structures around Britain at the end of the 19th century, but the practice was originally a Dutch invention going back many centuries. The idea was to entice ducks to swim into a netted tunnel until they were trapped in a narrow channel at the end. Decoy ducks (both model ones and real, tame ones) were used, but a dog made the whole process more effective. These dogs worked in an intriguing and unusual way. Instead of trying to catch the ducks, they would attempt to lure them into the tunnel by jumping, playing and generally messing about to attract attention. Similar behaviour has been observed in foxes, who will frolic at the water's edge, which draws the ducks towards them. It's not entirely clear why ducks are attracted to these antics, but they may be trying to drive the predator away or just keep an eye on it.

The arrival of shotguns made all of this palaver a bit unnecessary and this once innovative hunting method quickly went into decline. There are now only two breeds of dog in the world who can claim a duck decoy heritage; the Nova Scotia Duck Tolling Retriever from Canada, which is descended from European dogs, and the Dutch Kooikerhondje. There are about 100 duck decoys in the Netherlands today (a handful of these structures have also survived in the UK). These days, they are used as a humane way to capture birds so that they can be ringed and monitored for scientific and conservation purposes and the Kooikerhondje is still sometimes called in to assist.

NOTHING BUT A HOUND DOG

A trail by sight or by scent

The term hound comes from the Old English word 'hund', which meant any type of dog (as it still does in German). By the 12th century the word had taken on a more specific meaning and was used to describe a dog that hunts by pursuing game. Organised hunting really took off in Medieval Europe, but these hunting dogs were by no means the first hounds in history. In fact, some of the earliest depictions of dogs from the ancient civilizations of Egypt and the Middle East look remarkably similar to some of the hound breeds that are with us today. Hounds are often divided into two main groups; those that hunt by sight (which tend to have pointed muzzles, lean bodies and long legs) and those that hunt by scent (often with long, floppy ears and a fondness for howling). The word hound has come to mean dogged persistence, and not always in a positive way (nobody wants to feel hounded). Nevertheless, this appealing group of dogs isn't likely to be hounded out of our affections anytime soon.

PETS OF THE PHARAOHS

The Ancient Egyptians did some things we don't really go in for any more; mummifying the dead, for instance, or worshipping dung beetles. Nevertheless, modern life has more in common with the time of the Pharaohs than many of us realise. They played board games, for a start, and did wonders with eyeliner. They also kept pets. We know this because these highly sophisticated people left us an extensive record of the animals in their lives; statues, paintings, tombs, mummies, hieroglyphics and dog collars – yes, dog collars.

Now, some of these animals were more symbolic than real and some were rather brutally sacrificed to the gods (not something, thankfully, that the modern pet has to worry about), but the Ancient Egyptians did have a relationship with individual animals that resembles something like our attachment to pets today. Pets had names and their passing was mourned. Egyptians were really cat people and are often credited with making the wild feline into a domestic friend as well as a much revered goddess. But dogs also had their part to play in Egyptian life. Pet dogs were depicted in domestic settings and there are some remarkably realistic representations of hunting dogs – which is where our hounds come in.

Much Egyptian art depicts a highly stylised version of the natural world, but there are also many life-like images of hunting dogs with a similar appearance to Greyhound-type sighthounds that we would recognise today: a long nose, a lean body and legs that look like they're built for speed. The names of around eighty of these dogs have been passed down the millennia on inscriptions; Brave One, Reliable, Northwind, Antelope and one dog called Useless (who probably didn't really want its reputation to last for several thousand years). When these dogs died they were often mummified, buried and given a proper send off into the afterlife. It might not be quite what we're used to these days, but if a Pharaoh were to be magically transported into the modern age, they wouldn't be completely baffled by how much we dote on our pets.

FOOLED BY APPEARANCES

There is breed of dog with us today whose name suggests great antiquity; the Pharaoh Hound. A very majestic-looking dog it is, too, and it bears more than a passing resemblance to the Ancient Egyptian god of mummification, Anubis (who was actually a jackal). The story goes that a British woman came across one of these living relics on Malta in the 1960s (where they were used to hunt rabbits) and was so impressed she set about bringing the great-great-granddogs of the pPharaohs to the world's attention. It's not uncommon for aficionados of one breed or another to claim an ancient heritage for their chosen canine, but the truth is, sadly, a little less romantic. DNA analysis of Pharaoh Hounds has revealed that they are, indeed, a relatively recent creation.

No breed of dog has a pure, unbroken line of ancestry going back thousands (or even hundreds) of years. It's true that today's Salukis or Greyhounds look a lot like the figures on a Mesopotamian mural or a Roman mosaic, but they are in reality no more closely related to hounds of the ancient world than any other breed of dog, a Scottish Terrier, say, or a Pug. No breed of dog has developed in isolation so they are all the result of cross-breeding somewhere down the line. Types of dogs are made and remade in different ages and breeders in modern times have re-created old-looking types by simply selecting for the desired characteristics. Dogs intended for similar functions (speed, for example, or cuteness) are likely to share characteristics (long legs or fluffy coats) whatever historical period they live in.

Ten Hound Histories

1. *Afghan Hound*: This silky-haired dog with catwalk model looks was once a hardy hunting dog used to hunt hare, deer and even leopards. The Afghan Hound is related to other ancient sighthounds from the Middle East and Central Asia, such as the Saluki, and may have arrived in Afghanistan along the well-developed trade routes that existed in the region centuries ago. The Afghan is much hairier than other sighthounds, making it better suited to hunting in the cold, mountainous regions of its native country. The Afghan Hound was unknown in the Western world until the 19th century. The breed was first brought into the UK in the 1890s by British officers returning from a tour of duty on what was then the Indian-Afghanistan border. They were first exhibited in 1907 at Crystal Palace under the breed name 'Oriental Dog'. With their striking appearance and human-like hairdos, Afghan Hounds have often found themselves in front of the camera alongside fashion models and film stars.

2. *Greyhound*: These amazing canine athletes are capable of speeds of over 40 mph over short distances. Greyhound-type dogs have been used for hunting in Britain since the Middle Ages and were considered to be the hunting companions of kings and nobles. With the invention of the mechanical lure in America in 1912, commercial Greyhound racing began. It took off in Britain in the 1930s and became one of the most popular spectator sports in the country. Unfortunately, the welfare of Greyhounds has not always been the first concern of the racing industry, and many dogs have been discarded at the end of their racing careers – usually between three and five years of age. In recent times, Greyhounds have been the subject of much animal welfare campaigning. Unfortunately, approximately 1500 Greyhounds are still put to sleep annually in Great Britain when they finish racing, although many more ex-racers are now finding loving homes.

3. **Whippet**: Much smaller than the Greyhound, the Whippet is nonetheless capable of speeds of around 35 mph. These diminutive sighthounds were originally kept by working people to catch rabbits for dinner. During the 19th century they became strongly associated with working-class communities, particularly in the industrial towns in the north of England. Informal races were held as weekend entertainment, earning the breed the nickname 'the poor man's racehorse'. Whippets were often much cherished by their owners and allowed to live inside the home long before some more well-to-do dogs (who traditionally lived in outdoor kennels). Whippets were even used to warm children's beds. These dainty hounds are still very popular pets and Whippet races still take place, although they tend to be much more organised affairs nowadays.

4. **Borzoi**: Sometimes known as the Russian Wolfhound, the Borzoi takes its name from a Russian word meaning 'swift'. Despite this dog's majestic, perhaps haughty appearance, they were once very much working dogs that were expected to chase after wolves. The Russian nobility of the 18th and 19th centuries led lives of extraordinary leisure and luxury and hunting parties were elaborate, ostentatious affairs. It was not uncommon for vast numbers of hounds and hunters to be transported by train to the best hunting terrain. Leo Tolstoy's *War and Peace* includes a memorably vivid description of a large retinue of hounds and hunters in pursuit of a wolf. This aristocratic breed barely survived the Russian Revolution (when many dogs of the nobility were killed), but a few had already found their way out of Russia, notably a pair given by the Russian Tsar to Queen Victoria and her daughter-in-law, Princess Alexandra.

5. *Irish Wolfhound*: This giant of the canine world has a history steeped in myth and legend. Celtic sagas tell of gigantic hounds and their heroic deeds. There's even a legend recounting how Saint Patrick's ability to pacify an angry Wolfhound persuaded a Druid chieftain to convert to Christianity. Irish Wolfhounds certainly look as if they belong in a medieval tale, but the modern breed has a somewhat tenuous connection to ancient history. Wolves became extinct in Ireland in 1786, quickly followed by the virtual disappearance of the dogs that had once hunted them. The modern breed owes its existence to a Scottish Deerhound breeder, who set about restoring the 'lost' breed of yore in the 1870s by crossing what he believed to be the last remaining specimens of the old Irish breed with Deerhounds, Great Danes and Mastiffs. Whether this amounted to the restoration of an old breed or the creation of a new one, is a matter of dispute.

6. **Foxhound**: Hunting foxes with packs of hounds began in the 17th century. Hunters switched from stag to fox because the deer population dramatically declined when many forests were turned into agricultural land. One of the earliest packs of Foxhounds is believed to be the Quorn Hunt in Leicestershire, which was started in 1696 and is still going today. By the 1800s there were several hundred Foxhound packs around the country and foxhunting became an essential leisure pursuit for the landed gentry. Hunting was never to everyone's taste, however, and opposition grew as attitudes to animal welfare changed. The first anti-hunting bill was presented (unsuccessfully) before parliament in 1949. Finally, after many years of often heated debate, hunting wild animals with dogs for sport was banned in Scotland in 2002 and in England and Wales in 2004. Despite this, there are still nearly 200 recognised packs of Foxhounds in the UK, although they are not allowed to kill foxes.

7. **Basset Hound**: This breed gets its name from the French word bas, which means low. The first mention of the Basset appears in a French text on hunting in 1585, although this could have referred to any one of a number of short-legged hounds that were used for hunting rabbit and hare in France. Basset-type dogs actually did quite well out of the French Revolution. The Basset's short stature makes it slower than leggier hounds, so it's possible for hunters to keep up with them on foot rather than horseback. This was ideal for the new republic, where horse-owning aristocrats were much out of favour. The Basset's slightly comical appearance has made it a popular character in comics and cartoons. The breed's most memorable public performance came in 1956, when Elvis Presley famously sang his hit song 'Hound Dog' to a Basset Hound (although the song is not really about a dog).

8. ***Beagle***: Like the Basset Hound, the Beagle was traditionally used to hunt hare or rabbit by hunters on foot. The precise origins of the breed are unclear, but the name is from around the 15th century and King Henry VIII employed a keeper of the Beagles (although Beagle may have just meant any small hound, rather than a particular breed). There were once even smaller versions, known as pocket Beagles, that were carried in hunters' pockets or saddlebags. Queen Elizabeth I is said to have had kept a pack but they appear to have gone into terminal decline by the 19th century. Beagles have been much more successful than other scent hounds as a companion animal and they are popular pets, particularly in north America. Their keen nose and compact size has also made them one of the most popular breeds for contraband food detection work at airports.

9. *Rhodesian Ridgeback*: One of the few breeds of dog to come from Africa, the Rhodesian Ridgeback is descended from crosses between dogs brought by European settlers and semi-domesticated local dogs (who had the breed's characteristic ridge of hair along the back). The breed is sometimes known as the African Lion Dog and was probably developed in South Africa as a game hunter (it is officially recognised as a South African breed, despite its name). In the 1870s, the Ridgeback was introduced into Rhodesia (now Zimbabwe) by a missionary and soon caught the attention of hunters. Rhodesian Ridgebacks have been used to hunt all sorts of large game, including lions.

10. **Basenji**: Another dog from Africa, the Basenji is sometimes classified as a primitive dog, rather than a hound. Dogs similar to the modern Basenji may have lived semi-independent lives alongside traditional hunters in Africa for many hundreds of years. They were trained as hunting companions and bells were sometimes tied round their necks so they could be sent into the bush to flush out game. European colonialists first encountered the Basenji in the late 1800s in the Congo region (they were briefly known as Congo Terriers) but the handful of dogs that made it to Europe unfortunately died of distemper. Further attempts to export the breed in the 1930s were more successful. When the first pair in Britain were shown at Crufts dog show in 1937, these exotic dogs caused such excitement that police had to be called in to control the crowds.

THE SLEUTH HOUND

Hounds have frequently been sent after foxes, hares and rabbits and some have brought down gazelles and hunted wolves. On occasions, even people have been the object of dogged pursuit. All dogs, of course, have an amazing sense of smell, but Bloodhounds are exceptionally gifted in the nose department, even by canine standards, and have proved particularly skilled in the art of tracking human scent. Bloodhounds can follow scent trails over long distances for hours, or even days, without ever being distracted by other scents along the way. Most impressive of all, they can track a scent several days after it's been laid.

The earliest references to Bloodhounds go back to the 14th century and they were originally used for hunting deer and wild boar. A new career path beckoned, however, as early attempts at law enforcement got under way. Bloodhound-type dogs, known as sleuth hounds, were used to catch sheep rustlers and poachers as well as raiders (known as Border Reivers) along the border between England and Scotland.

Bloodhounds have been used by police forces around the world to track fugitives and to find missing people, especially in the USA. In one famous case in 1977, two Bloodhounds successfully tracked down James Earl Ray (the man who shot Martin Luther King) following his escape from prison. In the main, however, specialist Bloodhound sleuths have had their highly effective noses put out of joint by police dogs with more all-round abilities, such as German Shepherds. The Bloodhound, it seems, can be a bit too one-track minded for the modern police handler.

IN THE LURCH

So-called designer breeds have had a high profile in recent years. It started with Labradoodles and now there are all sorts of crosses between this and that which have been given fancy names (Cavachons, Puggles and so

[9 6]

on). In fact, though, there's nothing new about deliberately crossing two distinct breeds with a view to creating a dog with features of both parents. Lurchers have been around since the 17th century and in all that time they've never become a fixed breed. Once known as the poacher's dog and long-considered to be the companion of rogues, the Lurcher has remained well outside the canine establishment to this day.

Typically, a Lurcher is a combination of a sighthound (often, but not exclusively, a greyhound) and another type of working dog. A collie-type sheepdog is often favoured, but terriers are also commonly used. The goal is to combine the speed of the sighthound with the intelligence of the sheepdog or the tenacity of the terrier. All sorts of combinations are possible in creating a Lurcher: Salukis, Whippets, Border Collies, Golden Retrievers, Bedlington and Staffordshire Bull Terriers are all potential Lurcher parents. Some people prefer to breed two sighthounds, say a Greyhound with a Whippet, and these crosses are sometimes known as 'long dogs' rather than Lurchers. Fortunately, Lurchers have come to be regarded with more affection than they once were and they make excellent companions – even for people who don't go in for poaching.

FAT DETECTIVE

The superior sniffing power of the Bloodhound has been put to use in a novel scheme by one water company in the south of England. Hector the Bloodhound has the very unusual job of locating big blobs of fat. A lot of blockages in water pipes and sewers are caused by congealed fats, oils and grease. Finding them is no easy task for a human, but it's all in a day's work for a Bloodhound.

DOWN TO EARTH

A good grounding in the terrier world

Terrier comes from the Latin word *terra*, meaning earth, which makes a great deal of sense to any terrier owner with a few holes in the garden. But you wouldn't get an Airedale or a Kerry Blue down a rabbit warren, so clearly not all terriers were originally bred to go underground. Some of them pounced on their prey on the surface. Most terriers come from Britain and Ireland and even the ones that don't, such as the Boston Terrier and the Australian Silky Terrier, often have ancestors from the British Isles. Other countries have also produced earth dogs to dig animals out of their homes, but they're not usually called terriers. The Dachshund for instance, is officially a hound, despite having a job description that's identical to many a terrier.

THE GRISLY TALE OF THE RAT PITS

If you sometimes worry that the modern world has gone to the dogs and wonder if the past was a more civilised age, then remember this; people once thought it was tremendous fun to watch bears, bulls and other animals being tormented and torn apart by dogs.

Thankfully, this was quite some time ago and attitudes to animals gradually became ever more compassionate during the course of the 19th century. Animals were given legal protection from this sort of cruelty in 1835, when the Cruelty to Animals Act was passed, and a number of animal welfare institutions were founded at this time, including Battersea Dogs & Cats Home (which was founded by Mary Tealby in 1860). But there's one animal that has rarely been able to count on human kindness – the rat. With dog fighting, badger baiting and other dubious pastimes off limits, rat pits became an increasingly popular spectacle. There were rat pits in many of Britain's industrial cities, with dozens in London. Rat pits were often located in a room at the back of a pub and punters would bet on how many rats a dog would kill in a specified amount of time.

Controlling vermin was a legitimate concern in Britain's teeming industrial cities, but rat catchers would turn their rodents over to publicans so hundreds of them could be dispatched in a single evening by eager little terriers. Some of these dogs acquired celebrity status, such as Tiny

DOGTIONARY CORNER

Dogged, *adj.* /ˈdɒgɪd/ Originally used to refer to malicious or cruel behaviour (negative qualities associated with dogs), nowadays to be dogged is to be very, very determined.

the Wonder, a Manchester Terrier who killed 200 rats in under an hour, and a Bull Terrier named Billy the Raticide, whose record was 100 dead rats in just over five minutes.

In 1850 there was an attempt to bring about a prosecution against a rat pit, but the magistrate concluded that the Cruelty to Animals Act did not extend to rats as they were vermin and rightly reviled by the public. Animal welfare campaigners persisted, however, and there were several successful prosecutions in the 1860s, including cases in which it was the dog, rather than the rats, which was deemed to have been cruelly abused. Although the dogs may have been enthusiastic sports, they were often seriously injured by rats fighting for their lives. The whole ratting scene had developed an insalubrious reputation. Another nail in the coffin for this unsavoury activity was the rise of the dog show (which also often took place in pubs in the early days). Dog breeders were no longer prepared to put their prized dogs into the pit fight and preferred to show off their dogs in a less-violent arena.

By the 1880s, rat pits had all but disappeared from Britain, although a few persisted in the shadows. The last prosecution of a rat pit owner took place in Leicester in 1912 and that was the end of a tradition we can happily live without. The dogs of the rat pit have not, however, been consigned to history. Many of our most well-known and best-loved breeds were once champions of the ratting world; Fox Terriers, Jack Russells, Staffies and Yorkies were among the types of dog most favoured. Fortunately, this grisly heritage is now behind them.

FROM RATS TO RIBBONS

All terriers have working heritage somewhere down the line, but a handful of them have left their past so far behind that they're classified as toys, not terriers. The little-known English Toy Terrier is one of these, as is the much more famous Yorkshire Terrier. Today's Yorkies are smaller and daintier than their more rough and ready ancestors would have been.

Yorkshire Terriers originally took care of pest control in the coal mines and textile mills of their home county and they were also stars of the rat pit. Somewhere along the road these little dogs went upwardly mobile and left the pit for the parlour. Having become adored companions of genteel ladies in the late-Victorian age, Yorkshire Terriers soon became more acquainted with the cushion than the coal mine.

ONE TERRIER NAMED AFTER A FICTIONAL CHARACTER

The Dandie Dinmont Terrier is the only breed of dog to take its name from a fictional character. Dandie Dinmont is a terrier-owning farmer in Sir Walter Scott's 1815 novel *Guy Mannering*. His dogs are all called Pepper and Mustard, depending on their colour, and are distinguished from each other by adding 'auld', 'young' and 'little' in front of their names. The character was based on the real-life James Davidson, who did indeed keep terriers that were all called either Pepper or Mustard. Although the type of terrier Davidson bred had probably existed for a number of years, they acquired the name Dandie Dinmont following the success of the novel.

THE WHISKY DOGS

Two breeds of terrier have become so synonymous with their country of origin that they are now immediately recognisable as symbols of Scotland. The Scottish Terrier and the West Highland Terrier (particularly when pictured together) instantly take you to the land of heather and thistle, shortbread and whisky. It all began in the 1890s, when James Buchanan came up with the idea of using a black dog and a white dog to market his Black and White whisky. The brand went global, taking the dogs with them, and in some countries both breeds are known as 'whisky dogs'.

Ten Terriers named after places in Britain

1. *Skye Terrier*: Once a favourite of Queen Victoria, this is one of five Scottish terriers and comes from the Isle of Skye in the Inner Hebrides.

2. *Staffordshire Bull Terrier*: These popular dogs come from the industrial towns in the Staffordshire area of the Black Country where they were often miners' pets.

3. *Manchester Terrier*: Another terrier of the industrial revolution, this elegant-looking dog was once a star of the rat pits of Manchester.

4. *Norwich Terrier*: These little terriers once hunted vermin on the Norfolk fens and they were also popular with students in neighbouring Cambridge.

5. *Norfolk Terrier*: This terrier is a drop-eared version of its prick-eared East Anglian cousin, the Norwich Terrier. It wasn't officially granted separate recognition until 1964.

6. *Bedlington Terrier*: This lamb-like terrier looks dainty but they once hunted rats in the coal mines of a town called Bedlington (near Newcastle) and were also used for racing.

7. *Lakeland Terrier*: This terrier is closely related to a number of other breeds associated with the Lake District in Cumbria, including the Patterdale and Fell Terriers.

8. *Airedale Terrier*: These are the tallest of the terrier group and they began life in Airedale, Yorkshire where they often hunted along the River Aire.

9. *Sealyham Terrier*: This Welsh terrier is not called after a region, a town, or even a village. Sealyham is the name of the estate in Pembrokeshire where the breed was developed.

10. *West Highland White Terrier*: This terrier from the Scottish Highlands is a white version of its close relative, the Cairn Terrier, and was originally a hunting dog.

ALL IN A DAY'S WORK

The working lives of assorted canine professionals

The majority of dog breeds were originally developed for one of two functions: to help protect animals we want to eat (by herding and guarding) and to help kill animals we want to eat (by chasing and fetching). There are also breeds that we've used to kill animals we don't want to eat, but don't want to have around either (badgers, for example, and rats). But it hasn't all been about sheep, pheasants and foxes. Dogs have had an array of occupations and offered a surprisingly wide number of services beyond the obvious dog jobs. They've provided snow transport and been carriage guardians and they've been mushroom seekers as well as bed warmers. From the Swiss Alps to theatreland, dogs have proved themselves to be highly adaptable and eager to be involved in whatever tasks humans have dreamt up for them.

THE SPITZ FAMILY

The connection between Scandinavia and Japan is perhaps not immediately obvious, nor is the link between Siberia and Korea. Yet there is a canine thread linking these places together – the Spitz breeds. Spitz is the term used to describe a group of dogs who share a number of features, including thick coats, prick ears and a tail that curls over the back (all characteristics perfectly adapted for life in cold climates). Most Spitz breeds come from either Asia (such as the Japanese Shiba Inu or the Korean Jindo) or the Nordic regions of Europe and America (such as the Swedish Lapphund or the Alaskan Malamute). It's not entirely clear where they came from first, but the Spitz family may share a line of descent going back many centuries. The group includes Arctic sled dogs, reindeer herders and bear hunters and comes in a range of sizes from the powerful Japanese Akita to the tiny Pomeranian.

Ten unusual jobs for dogs

1. **Puffin hunters**: Getting hold of a grouse or a quail is puppy's play compared to getting your paws on a puffin. These cute seabirds live on cliffs and are eaten in a handful of coastal regions in northern Europe. The Norwegian Lundehund is one breed that was developed to hunt puffins. They are amazingly agile and flexible and have six toes – ideal for rock climbing.

2. **Canal boat workers**: There's always a problem with rats where you have goods to load on and off, so dogs (or even cats) can be useful. One breed in particular is associated with the canals and rivers of the Flemish region of Belgium – the Schipperke, once known as the Belgian barge dog, was also popular with Flemish merchants.

3. **Truffle finders**: Truffles are very ugly fungi that taste absolutely delicious and smell (apparently) like a male pig. That's why female pigs have traditionally been used to snout them out. The trouble with pigs, though, is that they tend to scoff the valuable mushrooms, which is why dogs are often preferred these days. Virtually any breed of dog can be trained to find truffles.

4. **Fire safety officers**: A connection between Dalmatians and firefighters goes back to the days of horse-drawn fire engines. These former coach dogs would run alongside the engines, warning people to get out of the way and protecting the equipment. Some American firehouses still have Dalmatians as mascots and these dogs sometimes go into schools to help educate youngsters about fire safety.

5. *Faith healers*: We all know dogs can cheer us up when we don't feel well, but the Aztecs and Mayans reached for one to soothe aches and pains. Mexican Hairless dogs (or Xoloitzcuintli, as they like to be known) had mythical significance to the cultures of pre-Conquest Mexico and their warm bodies were pressed to painful body parts to draw out illness.

6. *Tree climbers*: We've all seen dogs in the park jumping up at a tree, furiously barking at a squirrel. This natural instinct has been harnessed by hunters in north America, where there are more arboreal mammals than in Europe. A number of breeds have been developed, such as the Majestic Tree Hound and the Leopard Tree Dog, to locate tree-dwelling prey such as raccoons and opossums.

7. *Monastery guardians*: Tibet has many monasteries and three breeds of dog whose main job seems to have been to keep the monks company and to bark should an intruder pass their way. They may also have played a part in religious rituals. There are no precise records detailing exactly when the ancestors of the Lhasa Apso, the Tibetan Terrier and the Tibetan Spaniel began living in close contact with monks, but the companionship is believed to go back several thousand years. The Tibetan breeds did not become known to the outside world until the late 19th century.

8. *Military mascots*: There are currently Shetland ponies, Kashmir goats and a Swaledale ram serving as regimental mascots in the British military. Dogs, however, also play their part. The Staffordshire-based regiment (now known as The 3rd Battalion The Mercian Regiment), naturally has a Staffordshire Bull Terrier as its mascot and the Irish Wolfhound does the honours for both the Royal Irish Regiment and the Irish Guards.

9. **Stage performers**: Dogs have taken part in theatrical performances since the Middle Ages but dog dramas really took off in the early 19th century, making celebrities of canine stars. A French play called *The Dog of Montagris* (about the exploits of an heroic dog) was among the most celebrated. Originally staged in Paris (where it ran for several decades), it was equally successful when it transferred to the London stage.

10. **Charity fund raisers**: From the middle of the 19th century until as late as the 1960s, collecting dogs were a common sight in Britain, particularly in London and the South East. The dogs had collection boxes strapped to them bearing the name of the worthy cause and they wandered around busy places such as railway stations Some were owned by charities (including Battersea), but some were privately owned and available to hire to anyone who'd fallen on hard times.

JOINING THE DOTS

Anyone could tell you what a Dalmatian looks like but what were they originally kept for? They don't work sheep or chase foxes, but they're a bit big to be canines of leisure. They do, in fact, have stacks of stamina – which is a legacy of their unusual working heritage. Travelling used to be a dangerous business, with highwaymen lurking at every turnpike, so dogs were often taken along for protection. Horse theft was a problem, too, so the dog was often left in the stables to raise the alarm while the coachman stayed at the inn.

By the 19th century, a dog running alongside a coach and horses had become a common sight. Initially, any dog that was up to the job would do, but gradually the strikingly attractive dog with the spots caught the public imagination and became extremely fashionable. No carriage of style was complete without a Dalmatian or two running alongside. The dogs would wait by a parked carriage, performing the role of an early car alarm.

Dalmatians and their fellow carriage dogs often covered considerable distances and regularly accompanied the London to Brighton coach. The age of the railway brought an end to long-distance travel by coach and horses and the Dalmatian faced redundancy. These handsome dogs had a future as companions, of course, but their working lives were more or less over. Still, that doesn't mean a dog can't have a hobby and some Dalmatian owners take part in carriage dog trials just for fun.

DOGTIONARY CORNER

Poodle, n. /ˈpuːdl/ The name for this breed of dog has acquired a derogatory meaning when applied to humans, suggesting a person who is unquestioningly obedient, especially in a political context.

MUNITO THE WONDERFUL DOG

There was once a dog so clever he could play dominoes (and win), tell the time and spell *London* in both English and French by selecting from letters written on cards. This amazing canine was the toast of Paris, a star in London and a favourite in all the major capitals of Europe. The remarkable Munito (who was not one, but a series of dogs) was owned by a showman known as Signor Castelli (although this may or may not have been his real name) and debuted in Paris in 1817.

Later that same year, Munito arrived in London. He was advertised as *The Learned Dog* with the promise that he'd be able to do sums, play cards and spell words. The act was an instant success and Munito and Castelli did two shows a day as well as being available for private hire. One member of the audience on at least two occasions was no less than Charles Dickens, who wrote about the experience for a magazine article. Dickens speculated on how Castelli pulled off these tricks and detected the aroma of aniseed about the showman. The correct cards could have been marked with scent and Castelli probably used a range of discreet verbal and visual cues as well. However it was done, it was a slick act that delighted audiences and turned Munito into an international celebrity.

This first incarnation of Munito was a fairly large dog of a water spaniel or Standard Poodle-type, but after touring Europe for a while Munito disappeared from the scene, only to reappear in 1827 as a much smaller dog – probably a Miniature Poodle. Munito's career appears to have continued into the 1830s and there may have been three Munitos in total.

Such success naturally sparked imitation and dog entertainers continued to be a draw for much of the 19th century, performing card tricks and other seemingly impossible feats. Of course, there was nothing magic about Munito and his fellow canine performers, just the odd sleight of hand and some very patient dog training.

JUST GOOD FRIENDS

A life in the lap of luxury

Keeping pets purely for the pleasure of their company may seem like a thoroughly modern luxury. In fact, though, companion canines have a longer history than many of the working breeds we know today. That said, dogs that didn't earn their keep were often an extravagance too far for many people so diminutive dogs tended to find themselves in palaces and grand houses. Of course, these days most dogs are first and foremost friends and lots of them are quite small, but what distinguishes the breeds classified as 'toys' is that most of them don't have a working heritage at all. Some of them might have caught the odd mouse or rat once upon a time, but they mainly lived inside and in some degree of comfort doing what all dogs do so well – being companions.

HONEY, I SHRUNK THE WOLF

It's hard to believe that the wolf shares an ancestor with both the Great Dane and the Chihuahua, but there's no denying the DNA evidence; dogs (giant and tiny) are all very nearly exactly the same. Still, there must be something a bit different to account for the fact that some dogs stand at chest height while others are closer to your ankles.

Scientists have discovered that a little bit of DNA, known as a regulatory sequence, is probably responsible for keeping small dogs small. All dogs (and other mammals) have a gene called IGF1 (insulin-like growth factor) which plays a role in their growth, but small dogs also have a variant in the part of the DNA which sits right next to the growth gene and may restrict their size. Thousands of dogs have been tested and this mutation appears in all small dogs.

THE FLUFFY LITTLE DOG
TAKES ON THE WORLD

There's a fluffy little dog from Cuba (the Havanese), one from Italy (the Bolognese), another one from Malta (the Maltese) and yet another from Madagascar (the Coton du Tulear). Then there's the Bichon Frisé and the Lowchen, which both hail from somewhere in the Mediterranean. These dogs are all members of the Bichon family and they probably have some ancestors in common. Not surprisingly, then, they share a number of characteristics; they're small, they're fluffy, they're very, very cute and they've never done a stroke of work in all of the many centuries they've been around.

So how did these petite pets with no particular purpose get about so much? The answer lies in human history and an early wave of what we now call globalisation. Explorers, empire builders and traders travelled the world looking for land and riches and took their goods, their culture and even their pets with them. The Bichon family are Renaissance dogs who became adored companions in the courts of France, Spain and Italy when those countries were expanding their horizons and exploring the world.

Strong opinions are sometimes expressed about which one of these breeds is the oldest and whether it was Spanish, French or Italian traders who took this version of the Bichon to such far-flung lands. It's been claimed that the Maltese is the original Bichon-type and is descended from Roman lapdogs or even earlier dogs which were bought and sold by Phoenician traders (who came from the Mediterranean coast of what is now Lebanon and dominated sea trade in the first millennium BC). We know that Romans did dote on fluffy little dogs and that the Phoenicians traded small dogs (as well as big ones) along with exotic spices and precious metals, but proving a direct link with the dogs we have today is a tall order.

We do know with absolute certainty, however, that the royals and nobles of Renaissance Europe owned, loved and adored fluffy little dogs. This is because rich people get their portraits done and there are paintings in galleries across Europe which show kings, dukes, princesses and courtesans with a dainty, Bichon-type canine at their side. The Bichon family has come down a peg or two since the heyday of the courts of Europe and anyone can enjoy the company of a fluffy little dog nowadays – although it's a sure bet that you'll still treat them like royalty.

DOGTIONARY CORNER

Pooch, n. /puːtʃ/ The origin of the word 'pooch' is obscure but it was in use in the US in the early 20th century as an affectionate, if silly, name for a pet dog.

FIT FOR A KING

Only one breed of dog bears the name of a monarch, and that's the King Charles Spaniel (Britain's only toy breed). Actually, there are two breeds (the King Charles Spaniel and the Cavalier King Charles Spaniel) but these two variants on a theme share the same back story. There were also two kings; Charles I and Charles II, both of them mad about little spaniels.

This wasn't an unusual state of affairs in royal circles. Small dogs known as comfort spaniels were *de rigueur* with continental aristocracy from the 15th century on and soon found their way into the British royal household. There were small spaniels at court in Tudor times, but it was under the Stuarts that they became most closely associated with royalty.

Charles I kept spaniels of all sizes, so naturally his children grew up surrounded by dogs. A portrait in the National Gallery shows Charles II as an infant with a small spaniel on his lap. It was the beginning of a long friendship. The second Charles was rarely apart from his pets and was so fond of them that the diarist Samuel Pepys observed that the king preferred playing with his dogs to attending to business.

The King Charles Spaniels of today are not necessarily directly related to the dogs of the House of Stuart (dog pedigrees cannot be traced as far back as far as the those of the Kings and Queens of England), but the association between Charles II and little spaniels clearly stuck. It is not entirely clear when the breed took the king's name. He died in 1685, but the earliest known reference to 'King Charles's dog' doesn't appear until 1790. When the Kennel Club first considered the breed for formal recognition in 1902, they very nearly opted for the name Toy Spaniel. It took the intervention of King Edward VII to have the royal name restored.

EAST MEETS WEST

It's not only European royalty who went in for palace pets, but the household companions of Imperial China remained a mystery to outsiders for a very long time because trade and other forms of contact with the wider world were restricted. It turns out that the emperors and empresses of various dynasties had been busily breeding small, fluffy, snub-faced canines for centuries. These dogs were given royal titles, had their own servants and were often depicted in art. Dogs of this type were eventually given the name Pekingese, although a number of other oriental breeds are also descended from the original Imperial pets.

The first Pekingese ever to step foot in Britain was given as a gift to Queen Victoria in 1861. The dog was called Looty, a rather distasteful reference to the fact that the dog had been looted from the Summer Palace when British and French troops took control of Peking in 1860. It's said that British officers found five Pekingese dogs guarding the body of an imperial princess, who had apparently committed suicide rather than face capture by foreign forces. This story may well have been embellished in the telling, but one way or another Queen Victoria was given a Pekingese whose portrait is now in the Royal Collection.

THE FRENCH HAVE A WORD FOR IT

The attention lavished on fluffy little dogs has given the French language the verb *bichonner*, which roughly translates to something like *groom, doll up* or *pamper*.

Ten dogs that have never ever had a job

1. *Pug*: These chunky little dogs originated in China and found their way to Europe in the 16th century thanks to traders working for the Dutch East India Company.

2. *Havanese*: These small, shaggy dogs probably emigrated from Europe to Cuba during the time of the Spanish conquistadors and became aristocratic companions.

3. *Löwchen*: Also known as the Little Lion Dog (apparently because of its leonine haircut), this now-rare breed features in many portraits from the French court.

4. *Coton de Tulear*: This little dog gets its name from its cotton-textured coat and a port city in its native Madagascar, where it was probably taken by French trading ships.

5. *Bolognese*: This Italian companion dog is said to have Roman ancestry and was a favourite with the infamous Medici family during the Renaissance.

6. *Chinese Crested Dog*: These unusual dogs come in hairless and powder-puff varieties and were made famous in the US by burlesque performer Gypsy Rose Lee.

7. *Chihuahua*: Named after a region in Mexico, these tiny dogs look quite a lot like the animals that were sacrificed to the gods by pre-Columbian cultures.

8. *Papillon*: These pretty little things with the butterfly ears were once known as dwarf spaniels and were often seen on the laps of the noblewomen of Europe.

9. *Japanese Chin*: Known for their feline fastidiousness, these dainty dogs were once favourites at the Japanese Imperial Palace.

10. *Toy Poodle*: Although descended from working dogs (Standard Poodles were once water retrievers), the Toy variety was developed purely as a companion.

DOGS TO THE RESCUE

Canine helpers and heroes

In addition to the jobs we have asked them to do, some individual dogs have gone above and beyond the call of duty and carried out spontaneous acts of canine heroism, sometimes becoming celebrities in the process. The natural abilities of dogs have also been harnessed by skilful trainers to give us police dogs, search and rescue dogs, guide dogs and other assistance dogs who can help out with an amazing range of tasks. Dogs have been trained to locate people who are lost or trapped, open doors, unload washing machines, load a shopping trolley and detect medical conditions. Thousands of people owe their independence, their well-being or even their lives to dedicated dogs who have gone that extra mile to help.

TO THE FRONT

When the First World War broke out in 1914, Britain had yet to establish a military training school for dogs. Germany, by contrast, had been training dogs for war work since 1870. The issue was finally addressed in 1917 when a dog training school was established at Shoeburyness in Essex. Some of the canine recruits were family pets donated by patriotic members of the public. Others came from dog shelters, including Battersea.

Once they'd finished a brief period of training, the dogs were sent to the front. One of their main roles was to deliver messages and supplies, a task many of them took on with great gallantry. Dogs were fast and nimble and a less-obvious target than human soldiers and could navigate terrain that would have been impossible for a person.

At the end of the war, many of these dogs were brought home by returning soldiers, as were a large numbers of strays that troops had picked up along the way. 500 dogs were housed at Battersea's Hackbridge kennels for quarantine purposes. The contribution made by dogs to the war effort was finally recognised in 2004 when the Animals in War Memorial was unveiled in Park Lane, London. The monument is a tribute to all the animals that were involved in armed conflict during the 20th century.

DOG SOLDIERS

The 1st Military Working Dog Regiment forms a vital part of the modern British Army and comprises handlers, veterinary officers and veterinary nurses as well as, of course, dogs. Around 400 dogs support military operations in a number of important roles. Working dogs are experts when it comes to detecting explosive devices and weapons and they are much better than humans at checking vehicles or buildings for anything suspicious. They can also track people, provide security on patrols and generally act as a deterrent.

BEHIND THE BRANDY BARREL

Think St Bernard and you probably imagine a very large orange and white dog with a gentle expression and a barrel of brandy around the neck, possibly emblazoned with the Swiss flag. Throw in a frost-bitten traveller nuzzled back to life and a child who is lost and found and you have the complete romantic picture of our Alpine friend that so enchanted poets, painters and travellers from the 18th century onwards. There's more than a grain of truth behind this picturesque vision, although the facts of the matter have become somewhat blurred by exaggeration and embellishment.

The brandy barrel, it turns out, is a myth (the last thing you need if you're lost in a snow drift is alcohol) but the substance of the St Bernard story is true. The Hospice of Great St Bernard sits high on the Great St Bernard Pass, near the Swiss-Italian border. Originally founded by Saint Bernard de Menthon back in 1050, the hospice is still operating as a monastery which offers a welcome to travellers. We don't know exactly when the monks living in the hospice began keeping and breeding dogs, but there are credible accounts of these dogs from around the middle of the 18th century. This was the age of the Grand Tour, when what we now call tourism was first taking off. Travellers came home from their adventures full of tales about Swiss dogs rescuing people caught in avalanches and guiding travellers who had lost their way. Before long, there were postcards and souvenirs and the first St Bernard celebrity – a dog called Barry.

Barry was born in 1800 and lived until he was 14. During that time, Barry is said to have rescued 40 people, although there's no hard and fast evidence for this figure. Nevertheless, there must have been something special about Barry. He was sent to Berne at the age of twelve so he could enjoy a quiet retirement and when he died he was stuffed and displayed in the local museum, where you can still see him today. There is also a monument dedicated to his memory at the entrance to the *Cimetiere des Chiens* in Paris.

Quite why Barry, in particular, became so celebrated is not entirely clear, but stories of selfless animals saving human lives were a firm favourite of the time. Edwin Landseer, the celebrated animal artist, tapped into this sentiment at the tender age of 17 when he produced a painting called *Alpine Mastiffs Reanimating a Distressed Traveller*. The painting depicts two dogs of a type we now recognise as St Bernards pawing gently at a young man with the look of a poet, or some such romantic figure, who is buried in the snow. One of the dogs is wearing what appears to be a brandy barrel and so a myth was born. Brandy was never actually part of the St Bernard story, although the dogs did sometimes carry containers of bread and other useful items. The brandy barrel myth seems hard to shake, but the true legacy of the St Bernard lives on in the Alpine pass of Great Saint Bernard, where they are still bred and cherished and their story is told in a museum.

A DOG CALLED LION

Along with St Bernards, the giant but kindly Newfoundland became a symbol of dogged devotion in the Victorian era. These hardy, strong swimmers were credited with saving scores of lives and were given heroic status in a number of paintings by Edwin Landseer. One is called *Lion: A Newfoundland Dog* and shows a dog looking out across a Scottish loch. Another is titled *A Distinguished Member of the Humane Society*, which honours a dog known as Bob, who was reputed to have saved over twenty souls from drowning.

THE GREAT RACE OF MERCY

It was January 1925, and the Alaskan town of Nome was dangerously close to a catastrophic diphtheria epidemic. This former gold mining town sits on the Bering Sea, just four degrees south of the Arctic Circle. Once a magnet for thousands of optimistic gold rushers, the town was by now in decline and the population had shrunk to only 1000, including one sole doctor. There were no roads, no railways and the last boat had left in October and the next one wouldn't be seen until the spring. Apart from a dog sled team that delivered the mail, Nome was almost entirely cut off from the world for the long winter months.

It was slowly dawning on Doctor Curtis Welch that a number of child deaths in the town were connected. He suspected diphtheria and called a meeting in the town to discuss what to do. The town went into lock-down, with schools and libraries closed and families confined to their homes. The only cure for the deadly respiratory illness was a diphtheria antitoxin or serum. Dr Welch had a small quantity of the serum, but it was five years out of date. He sent an urgent telegram to Washington D.C., and waited for news. The reply came that some antitoxin was available in Anchorage – but that was 1000 miles away.

A decision had to be made about how to get the much-needed serum to Nome. Aviation was still a novelty at the time and planes were very basic. Nobody had ever flown across Alaska in the middle of the winter. Dog sled teams, on the other hand, had a known track record because they were regularly used for the mail run. Planes were fast but unreliable, dog teams were reliable, but much slower. In the end, it was decided to go with the dogs.

The serum was taken by train as far as possible and was then picked up by the first of several dog teams who took on the daunting task of carrying the precious cargo over nearly 700 miles of postal trail, all the while making sure that the little bottles of serum didn't freeze. The journey was done in non-stop relays involving a total of twenty mushers and 150 Siberian Huskies, who had to cope with temperatures that were sometimes below -50° C.

This was the dawning of the newspaper era and mass media was just getting into its stride. This story clearly had legs and was quickly picked up by dozens of newspapers. Readers were gripped by this tale of life and death with rugged heroes, desperate children, freezing conditions, imminent danger and impossible odds. There were also dogs – tough, courageous, fast dogs who were the townsfolk's only chance of getting the vital medicine. America's media was holding its breath as the final musher, Gunnar Kaasen, and his lead dog, Balto, arrived in Nome with the serum package after an extraordinary five-and-a-half day journey. Photos and film footage were taken of the triumphant musher and his dogs. These accidental heroes became unexpected stars (eclipsing, perhaps unfairly, all of the other mushers and dogs who had taken part in the relay).

A few months later, Gunnar and his dog team travelled to Seattle to make a film called *Balto's Race to Nome*, which recreated the famous journey.

Both man and dog made personal appearances at cinema showings, to great applause. In December 1925, a statue of Balto was unveiled in New York's Central Park. It was dedicated to the 'indomitable spirit' of the sled dogs.

Despite their status as heroes, Balto and six of his team mates were sold sometime in 1926 and ended up as living exhibits in a museum of oddities in Los Angeles. The dogs stood in their harnesses for hours on end in a hot room while members of the public stared at them. Not surprisingly, the condition of the dogs deteriorated rapidly in these unsuitable surroundings. Rescue was to come, however, thanks to a visitor from Cleveland who stopped off at the side show in 1927. Moved by the plight of these canine heroes, he started a campaign to get the dogs moved. Money was raised by Cleveland citizens so the dogs could be taken to Cleveland Zoo, where they lived for the rest of their lives. When Balto died at the age of 14, he was stuffed and he is still on display in the Cleveland Museum of Natural History.

In the months following the Great Race of Mercy, commercial air companies began taking over the mail contracts and the days of the Alaskan dog sled delivery team were all but over. The legacy of sled dog racing in Alaska was revisited in 1973 when the Iditarod Trail Sled Dog Race began. The race has run between Anchorage and Nome every year ever since – much of it along the same route as the serum run of 1925.

SWANSEA JACK

Local heroes come in all shapes and sizes and sometimes they have four paws and a tail. Swansea Jack, for instance, became a celebrated hero of the docks in his home town during the 1930s – and he was a Retriever.

Legend has it that Jack saved 27 people from drowning in the murky waters of Swansea's industrial docklands. He is also credited with having saved several animals, including a sackful of puppies. Jack lived close to the busy North Dock, where children would often swim. In the summer of 1931, Jack apparently jumped into the water and dragged a 12-year-old boy to safety. This first act of courage received little attention, but a few weeks later the local newspaper reported that large crowds had witnessed Jack rescue a second swimmer.

These were the bleak days of the Depression, which partly explains why this feel-good story of kindness and courage was soon receiving nationwide media coverage. By 1935, Swansea Jack's rescues were in double figures and he had become something of a celebrity. Tourists queued up to be photographed with the famous dog and he was given a number of awards for his bravery. There were some sceptics at the time who claimed at least some of the rescues were staged, but these doubts were largely ignored by Jack's adoring fans.

Tragically, Jack died in 1937 after ingesting rat poison. Following a campaign in the local press, a collection was organised to give him a lasting memorial. Swansea Jack was buried on the promenade in Swansea in a public ceremony in the year of his death and his memorial stands there to this day.

DOGTIONARY CORNER

Dog biscuit, n. /'dɒg ˌbɪskɪt/ The first recorded use of the term 'dog biscuit' was in an advertisement published in 1823, several decades before the mass manufacture of pet foods really took off.

POLICE DOGS

Dogs have been a tool of law enforcement since the earliest days of the parish constable in the middle ages, when records show that a sum of money was allocated for the upkeep of the constable's dogs. Initially, dogs were probably more of a deterrent than anything else, although their tracking and detection skills were also put to use.

The first formally organised police dog service in the world was established by the Ghent Police Department in Belgium in the 1890s. The dogs, mainly Belgian Shepherds, were trained to track suspects and to seize and hold them when necessary. It was so successful that other countries were soon introducing police dog units. The North Eastern Railway Police became the first force in Britain to run a police dog scheme when they recruited four Airedale Terriers to patrol the Hull docks in 1908.

Trained dogs are now an integral part of policing and they are routinely used to search for drugs, firearms and explosives as well as hunt for missing people and track offenders.

THE MAKING OF A WORKING DOG

Police, military and guide dogs usually come from breeding lines selected for their natural affinities for these jobs, but it takes more than good breeding to make a sterling working dog. The training and socialisation regimes these dogs undergo have been crafted over many years. From birth until weaning from their mother at around 8 weeks of age, these dogs will experience strange sounds, sights, smells and textures, including dedicated social interactions with human carers. When they're old enough, these aspiring canine heroes are taken to work, schools, supermarkets, tea parties, beaches and rock concerts, so when they are active service dogs they are calm and collected in the varied environments they find themselves in. This act of careful socialisation with the human world

Ten amazing ways dogs help humans

1. *Doing the housework*: Assistance dogs have been trained to help out with all sorts of household tasks, including opening and closing doors, picking things up, turning things on and off and even unloading the washing machine, all of which makes it possible for people with disabilities to live more independent lives.

2. *Helping with the shopping*: Dogs can be just as useful outside as inside the home. Assistance dogs can help people negotiate town centre shops and supermarkets and can take items off shelves and place them carefully in a trolley. Remarkably, some assistance dogs can even get money out of cash points.

3. *Answering the phone*: Dogs don't actually answer the phone, but hearing dogs can be trained to alert deaf people to all sorts of sounds in the house or at work. Hearing dogs let their owners know when there is someone at the door, an alarm clock has gone off or a fire alarm is ringing.

4. *Giving confidence to children with autism*: Specially trained dogs can have a life-changing effect on families with an autistic child. A dog gives the child stability, routine and confidence in unfamiliar situations. Dogs are trained to work in a harness which connects the child and parent, making it possible for the family to go out and about safely.

5. *Detecting medical emergencies*: Some dogs save a life nearly every single day simply by warning their owner that they are about to be unwell. Medical alert dogs have been trained to smell dangerously low blood sugar levels in people with diabetes and tiny changes that point to an imminent epileptic seizure. They can then alert their owner and fetch help.

6. *Investigating fires*: Obviously it's not safe for dogs to enter burning buildings, but they can assist with finding out what caused the fire. Dogs go into the premises once the fire has cooled down and search for traces of flammable liquids, such as petrol, which helps investigators determine if the fire was caused by arson.

7. *Locating victims of earthquakes*: Search and rescue dogs are invaluable in the wake of an earthquake or other disaster. They can find people trapped under debris much more effectively than humans, simply by using their extraordinary sense of smell. They are also more agile and can cover more ground.

8. *Searching for missing people*: Mountain rescue dogs are called out when people go missing in mountainous or rural areas. Some dogs are trained to detect scent on the air to look for anyone in the area and other dogs are trained to follow the scent trail of a specific person.

9. *Finding bodies*: It may be something we don't like to think about, but some missing people are already dead. Search and rescue dogs can be trained to find them, even if they are buried or concealed. Some dogs have been trained to detect traces of human remains, such as blood, hair and other tissue.

10. *Helping people get on with dogs*: A handful of dogs have been trained as part of an innovative scheme designed to help people who are afraid of dogs. Cynophobia is an extreme fear of dogs and is particularly common in children. Cynophobia assistance dogs are trained to participate in carefully controlled classes, helping people overcome their anxieties.

continues through adolescence, when the dogs are under the care of experienced civilian foster carers or puppy walkers, whose job is to ensure the dogs develop into confident and attentive adults.

Around 12 months of age, just when they are transitioning into adulthood, these dogs are transferred to special training units and assigned human handlers. Here, they learn to perform their working duties, such as searching for weapons or human remains, tracking offenders through harsh terrains, or controlling a hostile crowd. Although in practice this training is exhaustive and requires skilful handling, the underlying methods are simple: channel the dog's love for working and reward them hugely for it. Play is often the name of the game. For dogs trained to find specific items, like drugs, cash or weapons, the scent of that item will be associated with playing with their human handlers.

Over time, they will associate the scent with these rewarding experiences and be motivated to search for those specific items. For service dogs, a whiff of a large stash of cash, the smell of a suspect on the run, or even the scent of cancerous cells can be their signal to get to work.

THE STORY OF GUIDE DOGS

The first tentative steps towards training guide dogs were taken as long ago as 1780 at a hospital for the blind in Paris, but it was the First World War that created an urgent need for innovative methods to help the thousands of men who were blinded by gas or had sustained other injuries in combat. Dr Gerhard Stalling, a German doctor who was working with injured soldiers, noticed that his dog seemed to be helping his blind patients to get around. Inspired, he set about establishing a training system to reproduce and develop this partnership. He opened the world's first guide dog school for the blind in 1916 and there were soon branches all over Germany. The first guide dogs in Britain completed their training in 1931. Initially, German Shepherd Dogs were favoured, but these days the overwhelming majority of guide dogs in the world are Labrador Retrievers.

DOGS IN MYTH
AND LEGEND

Canines of fantasy and imagination

The human imagination has conjured up magical cats, diabolical ravens, shape-changing bats, ghostly owls and mythical horses but the dog of mystery is less commonplace. The dog, after all, has always been an ordinary, everyday sight and is perhaps too familiar to spark unconscious fears or inspire supernatural tales. Dogs may be scary at times, but the threat rarely seems other-worldly. Dogs cannot compete with cats when it comes to firing up superstitious inklings. Wolves pad around our myths and legends with greater frequency than their domesticated relatives. Nevertheless, the endlessly inventive human mind has given us phantom dogs, godly dogs, saints with dog heads and canine gatekeepers of the underworld. Much of the folklore associated with dogs, however, is more domestic. One of the most common threads linking legendary dogs is the idea of fidelity – a trait we all value in our dogs and which makes ancient canine tales ring true down the ages.

ON THE THRESHOLD OF LIFE AND DEATH

Many apparently unrelated cultures around the world have come up with the idea of a fantastical dog which is connected to death and the afterlife. These dogs are sometimes huge and black with flashing red or yellow eyes and supernatural strength. They also appear as omens of death or guardians of places associated with death, such as tombs, cemeteries and the very gates of hell.

Despite their terrifying aspect and close relationship with death, these mythical dogs don't necessarily have ill-intent and often do jobs that are actually close to the tasks our own domestic pets take on – that is guarding and guiding. Watchdogs guard the underworld of ancient Greece and the entrance to the Hindu spirit world. Other dogs have guided the dead of Egypt and Mexico to the afterlife. Rather than suggesting something sinister, these symbolic canines may simply express a human desire for companionship on our final journey.

WHAT'S WITH THE FURRY FACE?

Cynocephalus is not a word that crops up much in everyday conversation and it's a wonder that we have need for it at all, given that it refers to an improbable being with the body of a human and the head of a dog. Yet these strange creatures do pop up in human culture from time to time and people have even believed that they genuinely existed.

The idea of human-animal composite creatures has been with us since the very beginning of human existence and dozens of animal-headed beings have been found in rock paintings dating back at least 10,000 years. We'll probably never know whether the creators of these images thought they were representing reality or something more symbolic. Humans with animal body parts, such as mermaids, centaurs and sphinxes, are a recurrent theme in mythology throughout the world. The Ancient Egyptians are particularly well known for their animal-headed gods, including Anubis, the jackal-headed god who is associated with the afterlife. But these are definitely gods, not every day characters you might have bumped into in downtown Cairo in 2000 BC.

One fifth century Greek writer, on the other hand, wrote about dog-men as if they actually existed. Ctesias was a doctor and historian who spent some time in Persia and wrote a number of books. One of his books is called *Indika* and is supposed to be a description of India, although Ctesias never actually went there himself. His account is full of exotic plants, fantastical animals and unusual people, including the Cynocephali, or dog-headed people. These people are peaceful and keep sheep and goats and wear clothes and howl instead of speaking. Ctesias was not taken entirely seriously, even in antiquity, and his writing was often dismissed as a work of the imagination.

Despite the sceptics, travel writers down the ages have continued to give descriptions of dog-headed people in faraway places (although, not surprisingly, never first-hand accounts). The Greek geographer Strabo thought there were some in Ethiopia, and his compatriot, Herodotus, was told of their existence in Libya. The myth was still alive and well much later when Marco Polo described dog-headed people living on the Andaman Islands in the Bay of Bengal and Christopher Columbus wrote about how he expected to encounter them when he arrived in the New World. Of course, he never did meet any dog-headed creatures and these fabled beasts remain as elusive as ever.

THE DOG-HEADED SAINT

Saint Christopher is probably best known as the patron saint of travellers. Often depicted carrying a child on his shoulders, this image of the saint can be seen hanging from rear view mirrors in cars all over the world. Less familiar is another version of Saint Christopher from an earlier Eastern Orthodox tradition where he appears with the head of a dog. The reasons for this are a bit obscure but one legend has it that Christopher was a dog-headed cannibal until he converted to Christianity. Another explanation is that he was devilishly handsome and wanted the head of a dog so he could resist temptations of the flesh. The dog-headed Saint Christopher probably represents an amalgamation of pre-Christian iconography with a newly emerging Christian tradition.

THE TRAGEDY OF THE WRONGED DOG

It's an old story but a gripping one. A prince goes off hunting, leaving his favourite dog to mind the baby. On returning, he discovers the cot overturned and the dog covered in blood. Assuming the worst, the prince plunges a sword into the dog's side. Moments later, he hears a baby cry and notices the body of a dead wolf. Too late, the prince realises he has punished his dog for protecting his child.

In one of the best known renditions of this tale, the prince in question is Llywelyn the Great and the tragic canine hero is Gelert, whose name lives on the in the pretty village of Beddgelert in the Snowdonia National Park, north Wales. *Bedd* is the Welsh word for grave and there is, indeed, a grave you can visit where the noble hound is said to have been laid to rest. The inscription on the grave tells us that Llywelyn was so full of remorse following his rash action that he never smiled again.

Prince Llywelyn did actually exist (he was born around 1173) and the name Gelert probably refers to a real-life Celtic saint from even earlier, but the dog stuff – that's an invention. In fact, it was a masterstroke of marketing that has kept Beddgelert firmly on the tourist trail ever since. At some point towards the end of the 18th century, a man called David Pritchard became landlord of the Royal Goat hotel in Beddgelert and came up with the ingenious idea of putting a stone in a field and letting it be known that it was Gelert's grave. All he needed to do then was generate a bit of hype about the faithful hound who was unjustly betrayed and wrap it up in some fashionable Celtic romanticism. Before long, Beddgelert had become a must-visit destination with Victorian travellers and the legend was depicted in poetry and paintings. The gravestone is still a tourist draw today.

But how did Pritchard come up with the story in the first place? He didn't invent it himself, he simply matched a well-worn tale to a specific place. The faithful animal motif had been popping up in European folklore since at least the middle ages and variants of the tale had been recorded in many languages, including Arabic, Persian and Chinese. Intriguingly, the hero of the original tale may not have been a dog at all – but a mongoose.

It's thought that this well-travelled legend started out in India. A similar tale appears in a collection of animal fables which was compiled sometime between the third and fifth centuries AD (although it may be much older as an oral tradition). In this account there is a Brahmin's wife and a pet mongoose instead of a prince and a dog and the mortal enemy is not a wolf but a snake. As the story has migrated around the world, the cast of characters has changed slightly and some portrayals are more bloodthirsty than others (in one German version, a knight disembowels himself when he discovers his error of judgement), but the essence remains the same; some animals are incredibly loyal to us but we humans can be quick to judge and prone to violent vengeance – a rashness that can lead to a lifetime of remorse.

SAINT GUINEFORT THE GREYHOUND

One variation on the faithful animal myth led to a canine cult that persisted into the 20th century. Guinefort was a Greyhound whose fate followed a familiar folkloric pattern. Left in charge of a baby by a French knight, the brave dog was mistakenly killed by his noble master who failed to notice a deadly (and dead) snake near the baby's bed. Filled with remorse, the knight laid the faithful hound to rest in a well and planted trees around it at as a memorial. So far, so old hat. What happened next, though, was somewhat unusual.

Guinefort's grave became a site of pilgrimage, particularly for mothers with sick infants who believed that the dog who had saved a child's life would help their own children. The dog was regarded as a saint by locals after miracles were reported. The Catholic Church was not so impressed with this somewhat unorthodox saint and the Inquisitor Stephen of Bourbon had the shrine destroyed in the 13th century and the cult was officially suppressed. But the people of the Dombes region, north of Lyon, were not so easily deterred and the cult of the Greyhound saint limped on until at least the 1920s.

THE PATRON SAINT OF DOGS

Saint Francis of Assisi is well known for his kindness to animals and many churches hold a day of blessing for animals on his feast day in October – a rare occasion when dogs and other pets are welcome in the pews. Less well known is Saint Roch, who is the patron saint of dogs, among other things. The French saint also happens to be the patron of plague. Legend has it that he dedicated himself to caring for plague victims until he himself contracted the disease. While wandering in the woods expecting to die, a dog gave him some bread and continued to bring him food and licked his wounds until they healed. St Roch (also known as St Roque or St Rocco) is usually depicted with a dog at his side and dog blessings sometimes take place on his feast day in August.

FAITHFUL BEYOND THE GRAVE

Many visitors to Edinburgh pop along to Greyfriars Kirkyard to see the grave of Greyfriars Bobby, the faithful Skye Terrier who kept vigil at his owner's grave for 14 years until his own death in 1872. The inscription on a nearby statue of Bobby praises the dog's affectionate fidelity.

It's a heart-warming story. It's also a myth. That's not to say it's entirely untrue. There was a dog who regularly visited the church yard from around 1864. He was a popular local character, winning friends in the area and making himself useful as a ratter. He became something of a *Cause célèbre* when legal action was taken against him in 1867 because nobody had paid his dog tax. When some prominent people chipped in to pay the tax, the story was covered in the national and international press. When Bobby died he was a household name and he was given a decent burial by the entrance to the cemetery. All of this is fact, but an important detail is missing – the supposedly much-mourned owner.

Nobody knew at the time exactly who it was who had inspired such grief-stricken devotion. Several people have retrospectively been named as Bobby's deceased owner, but we will probably never know who Bobby's original owner really was, or even if he had one at all. The fact is that Bobby was probably just a stray, not a mourner. After all, dogs often hang around places, especially if they don't have a home to go to and they've found a regular source of food and some kindness. In truth, Bobby was just an ordinary dog but the Victorian imagination turned him into an icon of canine devotion. It's this attribution of motive that turns the life of Greyfriars Bobby from an exaggerated story into something closer to mythology.

DOGTIONARY CORNER

Dog collar, n. /'dɒg ˌkɒlə/ The phrase 'dog collar' meaning something you put round a dog's neck has been in use since the 15th century. In the 19th century, it also became an informal word for the clerical collar worn by members of the clergy.

Ten dogs of myth and mystery

1. *Cerberus*: This fearsome looking dog usually has three heads, the tail of a snake and the claws of a lion. He guarded the entrance to Hades (the Greco-Roman underworld) and was responsible for keeping dead people in and living people out. The twelfth labour of Hercules was to lead Cerberus out of the underworld without using weapons.

2. *Laelaps*: This hunting dog had the power to catch any prey it pursued and belonged to the Greek god Zeus. Laelaps was sent to hunt down the equally magical Teumessian fox, which could never be caught. Zeus eventually became so confounded by the paradox of the dog that could catch anything and the fox that could never be caught that he turned the pair into stone.

3. *Sirius*: The Dog Star, Sirius, is the brightest star in the constellation of Canis Major. One Greek myth has it that Laelaps and the Teumessian Fox were cast into space where they formed the two constellations, Canis Major and Minor. The Greeks were not the only people to see a dog in the sky, the ancient Egyptians believed Sirius was the watchdog of the river Nile.

4. *Garm*: According to the Norse mythology of the Vikings, Garm is a huge, blood-splattered wolf-dog who guards the realm of the dead. Garm is associated with destruction, in particular Ragnarok, a great battle of the future. When the time comes, Garm will fight with Tyr, the god of war, until they are both killed.

5. *Cù Sìth*: Big as a young bull with the appearance of a wolf, this Scottish fairy dog is shaggy and often green. This canine grim reaper appears before a death and is similar to mythical dogs in other Celtic cultures. According to folklore, anyone who hears the howl of Cù Sìth should run for cover before the third cry. Failure to do so results in death.

6. *Cŵn Annwn*: Also harbingers of death, these Welsh dogs are usually white with red ears and they hunt in packs. In Welsh mythology, these dogs are not evil as such, but they guide people to the otherworld where the dead reside. It's thought that myths about mysterious packs of hounds may have emerged in response to the strange cries from flocks of geese flying at dusk.

7. *The Whisht Hounds*: These Dartmoor dogs (also spelled Wisht or Wish Hounds) are one of many supernatural Wild Hunts found in folklore across Europe that are sometimes known as hellhounds. These spectral hounds are omens of death and the legend inspired Arthur Conan Doyle's *The Hound of the Baskervilles*. In this story, the ever-logical Sherlock Holmes proves that the myth of the spectral hound has been manipulated to conceal murder.

8. *Black Shuck*: A native of East Anglia, this enormous, unnerving beast with fiery eyes haunts graveyards and is associated with storms. His most infamous appearance was during a great storm in Suffolk in 1577 when a Black Dog was said to have burst into two churches (undercover of thunder and lightning, apparently) killing a number of congregants and knocking over a spire.

9. *Barghest*: This phantom dog comes from the north of England, especially Yorkshire, and is another one of many ghostly black dogs to appear in folklore from across Britain. This one is also large with eyes that flash, but it has the additional power of invisibility. On top of that, Barghest is said to appear when prominent people die to lead funeral processions of howling dogs.

10. *Sarama*: Said to be the mother of all dogs in Hindu mythology, Sarama gave birth to Syama and Sabala, four-eyed dogs who accompanied Yama, the Hindu god of the dead, and guarded his palace in the underworld. Sarama appears in an early Hindu text where she helps the god-king Indra get his cows back from some demons who have stolen them.

A FRIEND OF A FRIEND TOLD ME

Dogs and other domestic pets often find their way into much more modern folklore, known as urban myths. These contemporary tall tales often involve something heard from a friend of a friend and tend to involve shocking or frightening details. One classic example has been circulating since the 1970s and has come to be known as The Choking Doberman. The story goes something like this: a woman returns home after an evening out and finds her pet Doberman choking to death. She rushes the dog to the vet's and then returns home. A few moments later, she receives a frantic call from the vet telling her to get out of the house. The Doberman was choking on a finger – and the rest of the burglar is still in the house.

THE DOG THAT BIT YOU

The phrase 'hair of the dog' is generally used to refer to an alcoholic drink consumed to ease a hangover. Reflecting the idea that like cures like, this figurative usage goes back to antiquity and may come from a belief that rabies could be cured by placing hairs of the dog that bit you on the bite wound. Folklore has it that dog saliva is also good for healing wounds.

THE DOG
IN WORDS

Dogs from pen to paper
and word of mouth

Nobody knows where the English word 'dog' comes from. There's nothing like it in related Germanic languages, which use something closer to 'hound' as their everyday word for 'dog'; as indeed did English itself until 'hound' mysteriously began to make way for 'dog' in Old English. Dogs, in any case, can't say words (although they can understand quite a few) but human language is peppered with phrases and proverbs inspired by our canine companions. Dogs have also often had a bit part in literature down the ages and sometimes even played a pivotal role in fiction. They've certainly had more than a walk on part in the lives of many writers, who often work with a dog at their feet. This close relationship has put real and imagined dogs on the page and on our bookshelves.

BABY TALK

Linguists have observed that parents tend to adjust the way they speak when talking to babies and small children. This is sometimes called child-directed speech or, less academically, 'motherese'. Parents often speak in a higher pitch than normal, use a sing-song intonation and a more limited range of vocabulary. Invented, nonsense phrases such as 'whoopsie daisy' and 'vroom vroom' are also common in baby talk. It will come as no surprise to most pet owners to learn that similar behaviour has been observed when people talk to cats and dogs. Pet-directed speech shares many features with child-directed speech and in both cases these speech patterns seem very instinctive. As highly communicative animals, we humans just can't seem to stop ourselves talking – even when the listener doesn't know what we're on about. Many of us not only talk to our pets, but even put on a silly voice to do so.

DOGTIONARY CORNER

Doggone, *adj.* /ˈdɒgɒn/ This American slang term has nothing at all to do with dogs. Doggone is a euphemistic alternative to God damn.

LET SLIP THE DOGS OF WAR

Dogs are often mentioned in Shakespeare's plays but generally not, it has to be said, in a positive light. The word 'dog' is often used as an insult as well as a description for bad characters. Iago in *Othello*, for instance, is an 'inhuman dog' and Macbeth is a 'hell-hound'. Shakespeare refers to dogs as curs and mongrels and describes them as false and cruel. They are creatures to be beaten and are also associated with chaos and violence, as in when Mark Anthony says 'let slip the dogs of war' in *Julius Caesar*.

Shakespeare did, however, give us the word watchdog as well as the phrase 'dog will have his day', which appears in *Hamlet*. There is only one named canine character in Shakespeare and that is a dog called Crab, who appears in *The Two Gentlemen of Verona*. The canine character is companion to the comic figure, Launce, servant of one of the eponymous gentlemen. Launce says he saved Crab from drowning when he was a puppy and takes the blame when the dog widdles in the home of the Duke of Milan's daughter. The loyalty here is much more from the owner to the dog than the other way round. We don't know if Shakespeare ever had a dog, but there's nothing in his work to suggest he regarded them with much affection.

PHILOSOPHICAL DOGS

Dogs are rarely accused of cynicism. Indeed, boundless enthusiasm is much more their thing. Odd then that the word cynic comes from the Greek for 'dog-like'. The original cynics were a bunch of philosophers in ancient Greece who believed that true happiness lay in self-denial and a rejection of social conventions. A key proponent of Cynic philosophy was Diogenes, who was often known as the Dog in his lifetime. He believed that people, like dogs, should live without worldly possessions and have no shame in bodily functions (the philosopher did indeed do things in public that he probably shouldn't have). Diogenes' nickname may explain why the cynics came to be known as dog-like but another explanation is that cynic philosophy was taught in an Athenian gymnasium called Cynosarges, which means something like 'the place of the white dog'.

DOGS AND DICKENS

Charles Dickens was a great observer of life in all its wonderful variety. Animals did not escape his attention and cats, dogs and other creatures scamper through his writing in letters, articles and novels. Dickens didn't actually get a dog until he was 30, when he was given a Spaniel called Timber. The experience was obviously a good one and he was surrounded by dogs for the rest of his life.

There are a number of named canine characters in Dickens' novels, some of them as vivid and memorable as any human character. There's Jip, a little Spaniel in *David Copperfield*, who walks on the table at mealtimes and barks jealously at anyone approaching his beloved mistress, Dora Spenlow. The equally loyal Diogenes in *Dombey and Son* shows a kindness towards his owner, Florence, that is often missing from her own father, Mr Dombey.

Most unforgettable of all Dickens' dogs, however, is surely Bull's Eye, who is companion to the cruel Bill Sikes in *Oliver Twist*. Loyalty is again a feature of the human-canine relationship, but this time it is thoroughly undeserved. The pair are rarely apart but Sikes hits and kicks the dog, a violent tendency that does nothing to dent Bull's Eye's devotion. It doesn't end well for either character but literature has gained a captivating canine central character.

THE DOG THAT WROTE AN AUTOBIOGRAPHY

Virginia Woolf is regarded as a highly serious writer known for her innovative use of stream of consciousness, which doesn't always make for an easy read. Her celebrated but difficult novels are probably not the type of thing you'd take to read on the beach.

But while reading the love letters of the poets Elizabeth Barrett and Robert Browning, Woolf found herself laughing so much at the antics of their dog that she was inspired to write *Flush,* an 'autobiography' of Barrett's Spaniel. Written in the first person, the book gives a dog's eye view of the clandestine love affair between the poets and their elopement to Italy. Flush thoroughly enjoys the freedom of Italian life and the contrast with the constraints and conventions of London society gives Woolf the opportunity to dabble in a touch of social parody as well as enjoying this sensual world from a dog's perspective.

Flush became Woolf's bestselling book to date when it was published in 1933 and the author was a bit embarrassed by its success, fearing it would damage her literary reputation. In the end, no harm was done and there is at least one Virginia Woolf novel that is a light read.

A DOG'S LIFE

If proverbs are any indication, dogs are not exactly highly regarded in the English speaking world. A 'dogsbody' is a menial worker of low status and if you fall out of favour you might be 'sent to the doghouse'. When we make a mess of things we create a 'dog's breakfast', when things go from bad to worse they 'go to the dogs', when we feel really awful we're 'sick as a dog' and 'a dog's life' is a miserable existence. Dog is also used to suggest an inferior variety of something. For instance, Dog Latin is mangled Latin and doggerel is silly verse. Dog violets are flowers with no scent and dog's mercury is a poisonous plant.

Ten dog characters in fiction

1. **Argos (*The Odyssey* – Homer):** In this Greek epic, Odysseus goes off to fight in the Trojan War leaving everything, including his dog, Argos, behind. Twenty years later he returns home in disguise and is instantly recognised by his old dog, who wags his tail in greeting and promptly dies.

2. **Nana (*Peter Pan* – J. M. Barrie):** The children's nurse in this famous story about a boy who wouldn't grow up is actually a dog and was modelled on Barrie's own Newfoundland, Luath. In the original stage version, Nana doesn't speak or do anything that a real dog couldn't do, but she is very responsible.

3. **Montmorency (*Three Men in a Boat* – Jerome K. Jerome):** Originally sub-titled 'to say nothing of the dog', this comic account of a boat trip on the Thames features a Fox Terrier called Montmorency. The dog adds to the general mayhem and merriment by getting into numerous scrapes.

4. **Edward (*The Accidental Tourist* – Anne Tyler):** Edward, a Corgi, is a pivotal character in this novel about the transformative relationship between a travel writer who is struggling to cope with the death of his son and the dog trainer he employs to deal with Edward's behavioural problems.

5. **Timmy (*The Famous Five* books – Enid Blyton):** Timmy is a mixed-breed dog (turned into a Border Collie in the TV series) who is the fifth member of the Famous Five gang in this series of children's adventure stories. Ever the perfect pet, Timmy is constantly saving the day and helping to solve crimes.

6. **Karenin (*The Unbearable Lightness of Being* – Milan Kundera):** This Czech novel is a tangled love story set in the aftermath of the 1968 Soviet invasion of Czechoslovakia. Tomas is unfaithful to Tereza, but the faithfulness of her dog, Karenin, runs through the novel, which presents the human-canine bond as a truly pure and selfless love.

7. **Pongo & Missis (*The Hundred and One Dalmatians* – Dodie Smith):** Pongo and Missis (changed to Perdita for the film version) have a litter of fifteen puppies, which are stolen by Cruella de Vil. Smith had Dalmatians in real-life and was inspired to write the book when a friend suggested they would make a nice fur coat.

8. **Bob (Dumb Witness – Agatha Christie):** In this Poirot mystery, Bob the Fox Terrier is held responsible for an accidental death until more troubling evidence comes to light. Christie was a life-long dog lover and the character of Bob was inspired by her own dogs and is dedicated to Peter; 'A dog in a thousand'.

9. **Fang (*Harry Potter* books – J. K. Rowling):** Fang is one of a number of pets belonging to Rubeus Hagrid, the keeper of the grounds at Hogwarts School. This giant, friendly dog is described as a Boarhound in the books and played by a Neapolitan Mastiff in the film adaptations.

10. **Wellington (*The Curious Incident of the Dog in the Night-time* – Mark Haddon):** The dog in the title of this mystery novel is murdered before it even starts, but that doesn't stop Wellington, a large Poodle, from being a key character. Fifteen-year-old Christopher (who has autism) discovers the body and becomes a suspect in the murder before turning detective.

MIND YOUR LANGUAGE

What's the French for 'woof'?

Dogs the world over speak the same language, but humans apparently don't hear it in the same way. This is how to say 'woof woof' in 10 different languages.

1. wuff wuff (German)
2. ghav ghav (Greek)
3. guau guau (Spanish)
4. gav gav (Russian)
5. wff wff (Welsh)
6. wan wan (Japanese)
7. bau bau (Italian)
8. blaf blaf (Dutch)
9. ouah ouah (French)
10. wang wang (Mandarin Chinese)

There are over 200 breeds of dog recognised in the UK and not all of them were originally English speaking. When breeds from non-English speaking countries are introduced, a decision has to be made about what to call them. Sometimes a straight translation will do. Perro de Agua Español, for instance, is simply known as the Spanish Water Dog. In other cases, an altogether new name is dreamt up. One example is the Mexican Hairless, which is called the Xolitzcuintle in its home country. But sometimes, breed enthusiasts seem determined to keep the breed's original name in its original language. It may be obscure, it may be incomprehensible, it may be impossible to pronounce, but at least it's authentic. See opposite for what some of them mean.

1. **Kooikerhondje:** This Dutch dog was once a duck decoy and its name means 'kooiker's dog' – a 'kooiker' being the person in charge of the lures and decoys on a waterfowl hunt.

2. **Shih Tzu:** The name of this long-coated breed has caused many a snigger. It in fact means 'lion dog' in Chinese, which is nothing to laugh about.

3. **Affenpinscher:** This flat-faced dog is named after the animal it resembles – 'affe' is the German word for monkey, while 'pinscher' denotes a terrier-like dog.

4. **Schipperke:** This Belgian dog once worked on canal boats and its name means 'little skipper' in Flemish.

5. **Shiba Inu:** The name of this foxy-faced dog might sound exotic, but it just means 'little dog' in Japanese.

6. **Schnauzer:** This multi-purpose German breed has a magnificent beard and its name is apt – 'schnauzer' is the German word for snout or muzzle.

7. **Papillon:** The name of this pretty little dog perfectly describes the shape of the breed's ears. Papillon is French for butterfly.

8. **Dachshund:** Made up of the German words for 'badger' and 'dog', Dachshunds are actually known as Dackels in Germany.

9. **Shar Pei:** The name of this wrinkly dog is an anglicised version of its Chinese name and means 'sand skin'.

10. **Poodle:** Not an obscure breed, but a name with an unfamiliar origin. Poodle comes from the German word 'pudel', which originally meant 'to splash'.

THE DOG
IN PICTURES

From rough sketches to screen icons

From cave paintings to CGI, dogs have always had their place in the visual arts. Representations of dogs were often connected to religious belief in the ancient world and they continued to have a symbolic significance well into the Renaissance. A passion for hunting took off in the Middle Ages and images of hunting hounds were everywhere from manuscripts to tapestries. Dogs of every shape and size also started appearing in portraits alongside their proud owners and by the 19th century there were artists who specialised in pet portraiture. Even the most *avant-garde* artists have found space on the canvas for contemporary canines. Dogs have long been a firm favourite in comic strips and cartoons while cinema has turned a number of real dogs into superstars. Now, in the era of the instant image, we can capture and share pictures of our canine friends more easily than ever before.

BEGGING FROM THE LAST SUPPER TABLE

The Bible has little to say about dogs. The few references there are reflect a largely negative view (the dog that returns to its vomit being but one of the more vivid examples). Yet these ungodly animals pop up in numerous Renaissance paintings with decidedly religious themes. There's a small white dog in Titian's *The Archangel Gabriel and Tobias* and a fluffy little dog sits calmly in Carpaccio's *Vision of St Augustine*. Dogs also appear frequently in depictions of the Last Supper. Earlier Christians may have been shocked to see an unclean animal in such a sacred scene, but dogs had become a fact of everyday life in Renaissance Italy and added a touch of domestic realism to biblical scenes, despite their absence from the original source material. The dog which in early Christianity had been associated with danger, disease or even the devil was giving way to a dog that was both useful as a hunter and faithful as a companion. Dogs in Renaissance art reflected shifting symbolism as well as changing attitudes to real-life dogs.

PICTURE ME

It's amazing how many dogs there are in art galleries. Not looking at the paintings, of course (dogs are generally underwhelmed by anything that doesn't smell) but actually in the frame, especially in portraits. By and large dogs are not centre canvas, but look to the side of the main subject of a portrait, or maybe at their feet, and very often you'll find a dog.

One early and very well-known example is *The Arnolfini Portrait*, which was painted by the Flemish artist Jan van Eyck in 1434. The painting shows an Italian merchant with his wife and every aspect of the work, from the mirror to the open window and the bedpost, has been examined for possible connotations. Standing between the couple is a very realistic little terrier-like dog, which is there, so the art historians tell us, to suggest marital fidelity.

This painting reflects a trend for putting dogs into portraits which began in the 15th century and has never really stopped. There must be something about having a dog at your side which makes you seem more trustworthy. Dogs underline the fidelity of whoever is in the portrait, whether it's the faithfulness of a wife to her husband, a noble to his queen or a king to his subjects. Loyalty is not the only message a dog can bring to a portrait; while dogs symbolise devotion, they positively scream wealth. The well-kept pack of hounds or the lapdog in a luxury collar tell the world that these are people of standing. Dogs were also used as a device to mirror other character qualities of the sitter; a large Mastiff suggesting strength and courage, for example, or a graceful Greyhound hinting at nobility and a fine pedigree.

Symbolism aside, right from the beginning it seems likely that people also posed with their pets just because they really liked them. In the 19th century, pet-keeping became less of an extravagance and more of an everyday occurrence so dogs lost some of their symbolic function but not their popularity in portraits. This shift is clearly apparent in the many images of Queen Victoria which include not just one but often a whole gang of dogs without a hint of pomp or grandeur. She wasn't trying to emphasise her loyalty to empire, she just really liked dogs.

This tone continues in a painting of Queen Elizabeth II by Michael Leonard, which hangs in the National Portrait Gallery. One in a long line of royal portraits depicting a monarch with a dog, the queen sits with her Corgi, Spark, at her side – they are both smiling. There is nothing symbolic about this scene, it's just a warm portrayal of a perfectly ordinary domestic companionship.

ONE MAN AND HIS LAPDOG

Generally speaking, dogs in portraits reflect the gender stereotypes of their age. Men have hunting hounds and gundogs. Women have pretty little dainty things on their laps. But then along comes Federico Gonzaga, the

Duke of Mantua; a man clearly comfortable enough with his masculinity to have himself painted with a sword in one hand and a Maltese in the other.

The Duke was a patron of the arts and had his portrait painted a number of times by Titian, including one painted in 1529 (on display at the Prado Museum in Madrid) which includes a type of dog previously associated more or less exclusively with women. Federico was a dog lover who is said to have had over 100 during his lifetime. In this portrait he rests his hand affectionately on a small, fluffy dog and the pair are clearly fond of each other. The duke was involved in some complex matrimonial negotiations when this portrait was being planned and the dog offers the promise of marital fidelity. It was also probably his favourite pet at the time.

DOGTIONARY CORNER

Lapdog, n. /læpdɒg/ Used to describe a small dog, the term 'lapdog' has been around since the late 17th century and was often used to refer to the canine companion of a lady. It can also be an insulting way of describing someone who is sycophantic or subservient.

PUGNACIOUS ON THE PAGE

William Hogarth was an 18th century painter, engraver and satirist, famous for works such as *The Rake's Progress*, *Gin Lane* and *The Four Stages of Cruelty*, which were biting social critiques of the foibles of the age. He also kept Pugs. He had two, in fact, called Pug and Trump, and they were often models for his work. Most famously, Trump features in the 1745 self-portrait *The Painter and his Pug*, which is in the Tate Britain gallery. Trump bears more than a passing resemblance to his owner and his central presence in the painting serves to emphasise Hogarth's own pugnacious personality.

PORTRAIT OF THE DOG ARTIST

Sir Edwin Landseer is perhaps best known for the four bronze lion statues which guard Nelson's Column in London's Trafalgar Square. By the time the lions were put in place in 1867, Landseer was one of best-known and most-loved artists of his age. His fame and popularity came about in no small part thanks to dogs. In particular, Queen Victoria's dogs.

Born in 1802 into an artistic family, Landseer began drawing dogs when he was a small child. As an adult, he embarked on a career as animal painter to the aristocracy. Things were going pretty well, but then he landed the job that would really make his career. In 1836 he was commissioned to paint the portrait of one very special King Charles Spaniel; Dash, cherished companion of the young Victoria. A year later, Victoria became queen.

Landseer went on to produce numerous portraits of the queen's much loved dogs and became one of the most significant dog artists of all time. Landseer's dogs are centre stage, close-up and personal. These dogs are not symbolic, they are realistically portrayed as individuals in their own right – just like people. Dismissed as anthropomorphic and sentimental by some critics, Landseer's work nevertheless chimed with the spirit of his age and tens of thousands of reproductions were sold.

Victorians were not as embarrassed by sentimentality as people tend to be today and Landseer had an instinct for which buttons to press to get his audience reaching for a lace handkerchief. *The Old Shepherd's Chief Mourner*, is one fine example. A sad-looking sheepdog rests its head at the foot of his master's coffin. *Attachment* has a similar tear-jerking quality. A lost traveller lies on a mountain top while a dog mournfully paws at his lifeless body. Landseer may be guilty of projecting human emotions onto animals, but his paintings give dogs personality and dignity, which goes a long way to explain their enduring appeal.

A COAT OF PAWS

A dog on a coat of arms tells you something. Of course it does; every single thing on a coat of arms tells you something, providing, that is, you are able to decode the arcane language of heraldry. Coats of arms first came about as a form of identification for medieval knights and are still regulated by the college of arms. Animals of all sorts, real and imagined, feature frequently in coats of arms and dogs are a popular choice. Dogs mean loyalty, courage, vigilance and determination. Mastiffs, Talbot Hounds and Greyhounds are traditional favourites.

THOROUGHLY MODERNIST SAUSAGE DOGS

Every generation of artists tries to shake things up a bit and do something new, but dogs were just as popular with 20th century artists as they ever were. Pablo Picasso kicked things off at the top of the 20th century with a decidedly unconventional approach to representing the world. There were people with eyes in odd places and limbs at funny angles. There were oddly shaped dogs in his work, too, as well as in his life. Picasso had numerous pets throughout his life and one of his favourite dogs was a Dachshund called Lump. The pair first met in 1957 and Lump was soon making himself comfortable at the artist's home in Cannes. That same year, Picasso began a series of 58 reinterpretations of Velázquez's masterpiece, Las Meninas – which depicts a scene at the court of King Philip IV of Spain and features a Mastiff-type dog. In Picasso's versions, little Lump takes the place of the more imposing Mastiff of the original.

Picasso was by no means the only modern artist to be entranced by Dachshunds. American pop artist Andy Warhol acquired Archie, a Dachshund puppy, in the 1970s. Archie was soon joined by Amos and both dogs were the subject of a number of psychedelic portraits. Yorkshire-born artist David Hockney put his two Dachshunds, Stanley and Boodgie, at the centre of a series of 45 oil paintings. 'I make no apologies for the apparent subject matter,' he said, perhaps anticipating some sniffiness from critics, 'these two dear little creatures are my friends.'

DOGS PLAYING POKER

The image of a group of dogs seated round a table, smoking cigars and playing poker is a familiar one. If you haven't seen the original, you've probably come across one of many imitations and parodies. The dogs playing poker scene has endured for over a hundred years, but its creator has been virtually forgotten. The original artwork was dreamt up by one Cassius Marcellus Coolidge, the son of Quakers from upstate New York. He had no formal art training but became a successful newspaper cartoonist. In 1903, he started working for an advertising company that

Ten comic strip canines

1. *Algy Pug*: Rupert the Bear first appeared in a newspaper comic strip in 1920. Rupert and his friends live in the village of Nutwood and dress like Edwardian humans. Algy Pug is one of Rupert's best friends and loves practical jokes and outdoor adventure. He is not in any way dog-like, but then again Rupert isn't much of a bear, either.

2. *Snowy*: Fox Terrier Snowy first appeared alongside the young journalist Tintin in 1929 and the adventurous pair carried on getting into sticky situations until the death of their creator, Belgian cartoonist Hergé, in 1983. Snowy does talk on occasions, but he is essentially a real dog who sniffs, barks, chases, bites and cocks his leg.

3. *Snoopy*: Surely the most successful Beagle of all time, Snoopy appeared for the first time in 1950 in the Peanuts comic strip created by Charles M. Schulz. The pet of the ever-anxious Charlie Brown, Snoopy never speaks but leads a full and imaginative life expressed through thought bubbles and his typewriter.

4. *Rex the Wonder Dog*: Brought to life in 1952 by the artist who created Wonder Woman, Rex the Wonder Dog wasn't a mere sidekick but actually starred in his own bi-monthly comic. Rex is a crime-fighting canine with extra-special strength and stamina. Originally trained as an army dog, Rex takes on bears, tigers, dinosaurs and aliens as well as criminals.

5. *Krypto*: Also known as Superdog, Krypto is Superman's companion and made his debut in a *Superboy* comic in 1955. Krypto has superpowers similar to his superhero owner but often poses as an ordinary pet dog called Skip. When the occasion demands it, Skip turns into Krypto and puts on his Superman shield dog tag and, of course, a superhero cape.

6. *Fred Basset*: Fred the Basset Hound has been entertaining newspaper readers with his wry comments on human goings-on in suburbia since he first appeared in 1963. Fred's creator, Alex Graham, owned a Basset called Freda, who proved to be an inspiration. When Graham died in 1991, his daughter took over and the strip continues to this day.

7. *Dogmatix*: The tiny Dogmatix is companion to the enormous Obelix, who is Asterix the Gaul's sidekick. The dog first appeared in 1963 and quickly became a permanent and popular fixture. He is known in the original French as Idéfix, which means 'fixed idea' or 'prejudice' – a fact cleverly reflected in the English translation of his name.

8. *Gnasher*: Dennis the Menace's best friend is an Abyssinian Wire-Haired Tripe-Hound and he's been appearing in the Beano comic since 1968. Dennis and Gnasher have a similar hairstyle and are rarely apart. Neither of them are angels. The initial 'G' on Gnasher's name is silent and he is given to adding 'g' to everyday words, such as 'gnight, gnight'.

9. *Odie*: Odie is the Beagle who plays second fiddle to lasagne-loving Garfield the cat. The Jim Davis comic strip has been running in newspapers around the world since 1978. Garfield and Odie both live with Jon, their slightly geeky human, and they have a typical cat–dog friendship; Odie has no idea how much Garfield looks down on him.

10. *Dogbert*: Dogbert belongs to office worker Dilbert, who's had his own comic strip since 1989. Dogbert (who walks on two legs and wears glasses) is a very clever dog. He wants to rule the world but settles for taking a variety of jobs in management and technical support. Dogbert has become less and less dog-like as the strip has developed.

produced calendars, which is how he came to create a series of 16 paintings of dogs in human situations. As well as nine paintings at the poker table, there are dogs at the races, dogs in a ballroom, dogs playing pool and, perhaps most oddly of all, dogs riding a goat as part of an initiation ceremony at a Masonic Lodge. Some people find it kitsch, others find it just plain tacky, but few people call it art. Nevertheless, when two of the original paintings were put up for auction in New York in 2005, they went for nearly $600,000.

DOGGY WALK OF FAME

There have been dogs in films since the earliest days of cinema. Mostly they get walk-on parts, but there have been more than a handful who have successfully carried the starring role or at least made a good fist of it as a co-star. *Turner and Hooch*; *Beethoven*; *Benji*; *Air Bud*; *Marley and Me*; *My Dog Skip*; *The Incredible Journey* – the list of films with real dogs playing major parts goes on and on. But only three dogs are honoured on the famous Hollywood Walk of Fame.

The oldest of these is now all but forgotten. Strongheart was a character played by a German-trained police dog who emigrated to Hollywood and made it big. His real name was Etzel von Oeringen and he starred in a number of films during the 1920s. He was immensely popular in his day but has since faded from memory. Another German Shepherd Dog stood the test of time much more successfully. Rin Tin Tin was also an immigrant; he had been found in a bombed-out airfield in France by an American sergeant who took him back home to California. With a bit of training Rinty (as he was known to his friends) was soon working in silent movies. He had no problems making the transition to 'talkies' and went on to appear in over 40 films, making more money for the Warner Brothers studio than any human performer at the time.

The third dog to be recognised on Hollywood Boulevard is probably even better known. Lassie is the name of the character played by a series of Rough Collies in screen adaptations based on Eric Knight's story *Lassie Come Home*. The first one was filmed in 1943. It starred Elizabeth Taylor and Lassie was played by a dog called Pal. Several more films were made and a TV series started in the 1950s. The part of Lassie was always played by one of Pal's descendents.

These three dogs earned their places on the Hollywood Walk of Fame but they were all denied the chance to win an Oscar. There is no Oscar for animal performers, although it was rumoured that Rin Tin Tin won more votes for Best Actor at the first Academy Awards in 1929 than the eventual winner, Emil Jannings (who few people remember any more). There were also calls for an Oscar to be awarded to Uggie, the show-stealing Terrier in the 2011 French homage to silent cinema, *The Artist*. It was not to be, but Uggie was honoured with a Palm Dog award at the Cannes Film Festival.

NOT IN KANSAS ANY MORE

Fred and Ginger, Bogie and Bacall, Rock and Doris – all showbiz partners who made movie history, but Judy and Terry? Doesn't ring a bell? Maybe the names are unfamiliar, but any true film buff will recognise this quote: 'Toto, I have a feeling we're not in Kansas any more.' These often quoted words were spoken by Judy Garland to her canine co-star, Terry, in the 1939 film *The Wizard of Oz*. Dorothy's dog Toto is absolutely central to the plot of the film. If Toto hadn't chased Miss Gulch's 'nasty old cat', he wouldn't have been threatened with death by the nasty old Miss Gulch. If Toto's life hadn't hung in the balance, Dorothy would never have left the farm and ended up in Oz. It is also Toto who finally reveals the truth about the wizard.

It actually took longer to cast the actor to play Toto than any of the other cast members. The MGM Property department were asked to create characters as close as possible to WW Denslaw's original drawings for L. Frank Baum's book, but no one could quite work out what the shaggy little scribble of a dog was supposed to be. Roll up Carl Spitz, an animal

Ten animated dogs

1. *Pluto*: Unlike most other Disney animal characters, Pluto is not like a person. He doesn't wear clothes or speak and he behaves like a real dog.

2. *Spike*: This none-too-intelligent Bulldog often gets caught up in the middle of the never-ending cat and mouse chase in the *Tom and Jerry* cartoons.

3. *Tramp*: The handsome stray who falls for Lady in Walt Disney's *Lady and the Tramp* is best known for his romantic spaghetti dinner scene.

4. *Huckleberry Hound*: The blue dog with the bowtie and straw hat is totally tone deaf but frequently given to singing 'Oh My Darling Clementine' very badly.

5. *Muttley*: Paired with the unscrupulous Dick Dastardly in the Wacky Races cartoons, the bumbling Muttley is famous for his flying hat and goggles and his distinctive laugh.

6. *Scooby-Doo*: Just like his human companion Shaggy, Scooby is not very brave and has a very large appetite. He becomes a bit braver on production of Scooby snacks.

7. *Slinky*: There are a number of real dogs in the *Toy Story* films, but Slinky is a toy Dachshund with an expandable spring for a body.

8. *Santa's Little Helper*: The Greyhound was adopted by Homer and Bart at Christmas and has made many appearances in *The Simpsons*, mainly acting like a real dog.

9. *Brian*: A member of the Griffin family in the *Family Guy* cartoons, Brian is an intellectual. He is an unemployed writer and enjoys a drink (alcoholic) and dates (human) women.

10. *Gromit*: The wiser half of the Wallace and Gromit team, Gromit has no words but often has a much better grasp of the situation than his eccentric companion.

trainer with great Hollywood credentials. Spitz began training dogs for deaf people while still living in his native Germany and his skills at giving silent commands gave him the edge when he moved to the US in 1926 just as sound was hitting the movies. Trainers working in silent film could just bark out their instructions across the set, but new technology called for new techniques. Spitz was also responsible for deciding that a Cairn Terrier most closely resembled the dog in the original artwork and set about working with a dog called Terry (who was actually female). Terry was paid $125 a week (compared to Garland's fee of $500).

Terry certainly earned her money. She had to deal with terrifying wind machines on set and one of the witch's soldiers stepped on her, breaking a foot and putting her out of action for a couple of weeks. She did get to attend the film premiere and soon after changed her name to Toto. Dorothy and Toto – now that's a pair that rings a bell.

DOGTIONARY CORNER

Hound, v. /haʊnd/ To pursue, chase or track in the manner of a scent hound. To hound someone out means to drive them away.

BATTERSEA
DOGS & CATS HOME

The story of the one of the oldest and best-loved dogs' homes

The streets of Victorian London were often a miserable place to be a dog. Many were used to pull carts through the busy streets, others were stolen for ransom and sometimes even traded for their skins and fur. Dog fighting and other cruel sports were not uncommon. Dogs were rounded up from time to time because of rabies scares and the lot of a London stray was generally not a happy one. But London in the 19th century was also a place of radical ideas and fresh perspectives, which gave rise to questions about the treatment of animals. Battersea Dogs & Cats Home originated at a time when growing numbers of people began objecting to the cruelty routinely meted out to dogs and other animals. Once dismissed as a cause for soft-hearted eccentrics, The Home was a pioneering and inspirational institution that has become one of the best-known animal rescue centres in the world.

HOW IT ALL BEGAN

If it hadn't been for some disgruntled neighbours, Battersea Dogs & Cats Home would be known to millions as the beloved Holloway Dogs & Cats Home as this is where Battersea's founder, Mary Tealby, first set up her Temporary Home for Lost & Starving Dogs in 1860. Mary was one of a number of increasingly vocal campaigners who sought to improve the lot of animals in Victorian Britain.

The idea for the Home is said to have come to her when she visited a friend who had taken in a sick stray. Mary took the dog home with her and had an idea. What London needed, she decided, was a canine asylum – somewhere that waifs and strays could go to for food, shelter and some comfort. First of all, she took dogs into her own home, but soon she was looking for more suitable premises. Mary moved her Home into disused stables in Holloway, set up a committee and set about raising funds. Word soon spread and a steady stream of dogs in need began arriving.

Since the outset, a number of local residents had complained about the noise and smell coming from The Home. Mary and her committee realised it was probably a losing battle and that eventually they would have to relocate. Sadly, Mary Tealby died in 1865 and never got to see the new Home in Battersea, which opened in 1871 on the site where it still stands today. The location was ideal because the plot of land was sandwiched between two railway tracks so the Home wouldn't be right next door to anyone's home. The Temporary Home for Lost & Starving Dogs only just survived the death of its champion, but the remaining committee members pulled together and continued the work Mary had started. It's hard to imagine what any of them would make of the place today, but they would surely be very proud indeed.

Ten milestones of Battersea history

1. 1885: Queen Victoria becomes the Home's first royal patron

2. 1898: An epidemic of rabies in London leads to the opening of the Home's first country site in Hackbridge, Surrey

3. 1909: Two motor vans and six horse-drawn vans are hired to collect the strays of London

4. 1917: Dogs from Battersea are enrolled in the War Office's new dog training school

5. 1956: Queen Elizabeth II becomes the Home's patron

6. 1979: Battersea acquires Bell Mead Kennels on the edge of Old Windsor

7. 1984: The first full-time Battersea veterinary surgeon is employed

8. 1995: Battersea holds its first annual reunion in Battersea Park

9. 2000: Battersea's third centre, at Brands Hatch in Kent, is opened

10. 2015: Building work completed to replace Battersea's oldest Victorian kennels with four new blocks, each of 14 kennels.

WHAT THE DICKENS?

A home for dogs? What a ridiculous idea! This was the reaction of certain sections of the press when the Temporary Home for Lost & Starving Dogs opened its doors in 1860. Some publications just sneered sarcastically at the project while *The Times* published an editorial which suggested that the founders of such an institution must have 'taken leave of their sober senses' and that the Home was an example of 'ridiculous sentimentalism'. But then along came Charles Dickens. By the time Mary Tealby opened her Home, Dickens was firmly established as one of the most well-known and best-loved writers in the English language. Dickens had always shown an interest in humanitarian causes and spoke out on contemporary issues such as cruelty to children, slavery and exploitation of the poor. He was also a great dog lover.

In 1862, Dickens gave The Home a much needed boost when an article was published in his magazine *All the Year Round* which praised the work of 'this Holloway asylum'. Such approval from this very eminent Victorian did a lot to change attitudes towards the Home and its mission. The number of supporters, donors and volunteers steadily grew and the welfare of dogs became a cause respectable people could support without fear of ridicule.

DOGTIONARY CORNER

Puppy, n. /ˈpʌpi/ The word puppy may come from the French word poupée, meaning puppet or doll, and was used to refer to small dogs from the 15th century. The word later developed the more specific meaning of 'young dog'.

BATTERSEA BY NUMBERS

Battersea has three sites, employs over 300 staff and depends on around 1000 volunteers to look after nearly 6000 dogs who pass through our 480 kennels every year. There are around 400 dogs on site across the three centres and on foster at any one time, who are all looked after by six vets and a clinic team of 33 staff.

Eight hundred lost cats and dogs are reunited with their owners in a typical year and an average of seven dogs and seven cats are rehomed per day. The average stay for a dog at Battersea is 29 days. Battersea aims to never turn away a dog or cat in need and we take in thirteen canine new arrivals each day. All of this costs over £14 million a year.

SERVICE DOGS

Not all dogs in active service today come from specialised breeding programmes. In fact, some of these dogs are stray or abandoned dogs who have found their way into rescue centres such as Battersea. Not every dog that comes into the Home has got what it takes to adapt to life as a family pet but even dogs who are not suitable for domestic homes may have a new and exhilarating life ahead of them as well as a fine career. A number of universities are conducting research into the use of rescue dogs as service dogs, and have found them to be very able canines for innumerable service roles.

At Battersea, we have our own Service Dogs Manager who is trained to identify potential candidates for professional training with service dog organisations such as the Army, the RAF, HM Customs, the Police, Prison and Security Services as well as working sheepdog and gundog owners.

Ten extra-special Battersea dogs...

1. **Mary Tealby's first stray:** We don't know the name of this first dog, but it had been found in a terrible condition on the streets of Islington. Mary took the stray into her home and spent several days and nights trying to nurse it back to health. Unfortunately, the dog did not survive, but the experience clearly gave Mary an idea. Thankfully for the capital's many dogs in need, the legacy of that one hungry, neglected animal lives on to this day.

2. **The criminal's canine accomplice:** Notorious burglar and murderer Charlie Peace always took his dog to 'work' with him to act as a lookout and warn of anyone approaching. One of Peace's last requests before he was executed on 25 February 1879, was that his canine companion in crime be cared for. Battersea was happy to oblige and the dog came to the Home and earned his keep as a watchdog, living at Battersea until he died.

3. **Shackleton's sled team:** Around 100 dogs were housed at the Hackbridge site in preparation for Ernest Shackleton's second Antarctic Expedition in 1914. They were mainly Husky-type dogs and were to provide the main form of land transport on what was hoped would be the first land crossing of the Antarctic. Shackleton's ship became stuck in ice and the expedition was unsuccessful. Sadly, none of the dogs returned.

4. **Bootsie the heartbroken dog:** Mongrel Bootsie was found in Charing Cross Station back in the 1970s. He was guarding a pair of shoes and he refused to be parted from them. A policeman brought Bootsie (and his shoes) to Battersea, and he was eventually rehomed to a family in Bristol. His shoes were rehomed with him. Nobody ever found out who the shoes had originally belonged to.

5. **Peter and Paul the blind dog and his guide:** Blind Labrador Retriever Peter was led everywhere by his devoted companion Paul – even when they got lost. The pair were brought to the Home as strays. Paul nosed Peter in and out of doorways as they went down corridors and steered him around dustbins. He even guided him to a bowl of water in their kennel. Thanks to the publicity the pair attracted, Peter and Paul were reunited with their grateful owner.

6. **Dolores, the film star dog:** Spaniel Dolores went from being a homeless Battersea dog to film stardom with Rod Steiger in the 1957 hit *Across the Bridge*. Dolores played the dog of a Mexican criminal and she earned glowing praise from the *News Chronicle* reviewer, who called her; 'one of the most endearing bitches in screen history – a mournfully unthoroughbred Spaniel called Dolores, who was discovered in Battersea Dogs Home.'

7. **Lucky the two-and-half-millionth Battersea dog:** In 1983, a brown mongrel was found wandering the streets in Hackney and taken to Battersea. The dog was given a quick brush up, checked over by a vet and given the name Lucky. He was then presented to the press with a card around his neck with the simple message 'No. 2,500,000'. Lucky was in most of the newspapers the next day and was spotted by his owners, who had lost him six weeks previously. His real name was Scamp.

8. **Red the Lurcher:** This clever dog became world famous after he was caught on camera in 2004 regularly escaping from his kennel and letting out all his canine friends to share in a little midnight feasting. At first, Battersea staff were at a loss to explain how several dogs were managing to get out of their kennels at night and help themselves to the food supplies. The publicity generated by the footage of Red unlocking the kennels led to him finding a new home.

9. **April the Ambassadog:** April is a Staffordshire Bull Terrier who had been used as a bait dog before arriving at Battersea, where she received treatment for her injuries before being re-homed. She remained loving and trusting throughout, and is now a Battersea Ambassadog. Around a third of dogs currently coming into the Home are Staffies or Staffie-crosses and April is an important part of the Home's campaign to encourage people to take on one of these gentle, loving dogs.

10. **Herbie the Detector dog:** Springer Spaniel Herbie was one of those dogs who is more suited to a working life than living as a pet. After having been assessed by Battersea staff, an alternative future was found for him and he became a police sniffer dog with the Northamptonshire force. Herbie is highly successful in his new career and has detected several high-value hoards of drugs and money.

...AND ONE FOX

Freddy the fox briefly became a Battersea celebrity in the 1950s when he was taken to the Home by a member of the public who had found the cub lying next to his dead mother. The fox attracted media attention and drew crowds to Battersea. It was not, however, the ideal home for a fox so Freddy was re-homed by No. 12 Squadron of the RAF (whose insignia was a fox) and became a mascot.

NOT FORGETTING...THE CATS

The original Home was set up with dogs in mind, but Battersea actually began accepting cats as early as 1883, although the charity's name didn't reflect the fact until 2002, when it was changed to Battersea Dogs & Cats Home. Battersea now takes in over 3000 cats a year and can house 250 at any one time.

DOGTIONARY CORNER

Sea-dog, *n.* /siːdɒg/ Used as a word for a pirate in Elizabethan times, sea-dog later referred to any sailor with a lot of experience at sea. The word has also been used as an alternative to 'seal', but has no connection with dogs.

DOGS REMEMBERED

Dogs lost, mourned and celebrated

Sharing your life with dogs means wet noses, waggy tails, muddy paws, a warm welcome home and, sadly, loss. When people die, there are time-honoured traditions and formalised rituals which guide us through grief, but we're often at a bit of a loss to know how to mark the passing of a much loved pet. We may feel embarrassed at the depth of our sadness and taken aback by just how difficult it can be to say goodbye. Some people find the death of a dog so upsetting that they can't face having another one. But grief is the price we pay for unconditional love and we honour and celebrate our pets in our own way with poems or gravestones or cherished memories or whatever it takes to get us through.

A DECENT SEND-OFF

There have been dog burials for more or less as long as there have been dogs. A number of large-scale animal cemeteries have been found in Egypt and the Middle East dating back several thousand years, although the significance of these canine remains is not always clear. Why, for example, were several hundred sighthound-type dogs carefully buried in a dog cemetery around 450 BC in Ashkelon in modern day Israel? Did they die as part of a religious ritual or were they perhaps valued for their healing powers? It remains a mystery. Similarly, no one's quite sure why an astonishing eight million mummified animals, most of them dogs, were buried in the catacombs of the canine god, Anubis, at a site in Saqqara, Egypt – although some sort of ritual sacrifice seems like the most plausible explanation.

These particular dogs were obviously not pets as we understand the concept today, but the many heartfelt epitaphs to named pets on numerous tombstones from Ancient Greece and Rome testify to the fact that dogs were loved, mourned and given a formal burial a very long time ago. Back-garden burials aside, it took quite a while longer for the idea of a dedicated pet cemetery to take hold in the modern world. The pet cemetery which claims to be the oldest one still operating in the world is the Hartsdale Canine Cemetery in New York State. It opened in 1896 when a veterinarian allowed a friend to bury a much loved dog in his apple orchard. The cemetery is now the resting place of some 80,000 pets, including birds and reptiles as well as the more usual cats and dogs.

Older, but on a much smaller scale, is the pet cemetery in Hyde Park, London, which began more by accident than design. When the dog belonging to a family who regularly visited the park died in 1881, the gatekeeper agreed to bury the dog in his garden. A headstone was put in place with an inscription which read, 'Poor Cherry. Died April 28 1881.' Before long, an unofficial pet cemetery began expanding in the small garden and by the time the cemetery was closed in 1903, around 300 little headstones had been squeezed in.

Paris has a much grander dog cemetery than London, complete with fine art deco entrance gates and elaborate headstones and monuments to deceased pets. Le Cimetière des Chiens et Autres Animaux Domestiques (the Cemetery of Dogs and Other Domestic Animals) opened in 1899 in the north-east of Paris and is divided into four sections; one for dogs, one for cats, one for birds and another for other animals (where a lion, a racehorse, a monkey and some fish are among those who rest in peace). Probably the best-known dog among the 40,000 animals buried in the Paris necropolis is Rin Tin Tin, the famous Hollywood canine actor. The superstar German Shepherd Dog was returned to the country of his birth soon after his death in 1932 and interred in Le Cimetière des Chiens. Amid all this death, life goes on and the Paris cemetery is home to a population of feral cats who are looked after by a local cat welfare association.

DOGTIONARY CORNER

Bow wow, n. /ˈbaʊˈwaʊ/ This child's word for a dog is an onomatopoeia and was perhaps most famously used in the song 'Daddy Wouldn't Buy Me a Bow Wow', which was written in 1892.

TRIBUTE TO A BYRONIC HERO

The Romantic poet, Lord Byron, was never one for understatement. His short, eventful life was full of passion and scandal and his pet- keeping habits were as flamboyant as everything else he did. He kept a bear while a student at Cambridge (dogs were not allowed) and had monkeys, birds, a goat and a badger as well as numerous cats and dogs at various points in his life. His favourite dog was Boatswain, a Newfoundland he acquired when he was just 15. Boatswain died of rabies in 1808 and Byron built a monument and tomb for the dog on his estate, Newstead Abbey in Nottinghamshire. Byron intended the tomb to be his own resting place, too, but in the end the poet was buried in the family vault. The inscription on the impressive monument reads; 'Near this spot are deposited the Remains of one who possessed Beauty without Vanity, Strength without Insolence, Courage without Ferocity, and all the Virtues of Man without his Vices'.

POETIC GOODBYES

Poets are allowed to be emotional and some of our greatest bards have put pen to paper on the death of a dear dog. The Victorian poet and critic, Matthew Arnold, wrote a poem called 'Geist's Grave' when his four-year-old Dachshund died. It is long and full of melancholy for a 'dear little friend'. William Wordsworth, who gave us a host of golden daffodils, also wrote a poetic tribute to his dog, Music, who had 'a soul of love'. Scottish poet, Robert Burns was also a dog lover and wrote 'My Hoggie' about the death of his sheepdog: 'My joy, my pride, my Hoggie! My only beast, I had nae mae.' Flowery tributes like these have a long pedigree and are not restricted to poets. Nearly two thousand years ago, a Roman family penned these words on the death of their dog, Margarita, which were carved into stone for posterity: 'Alas, misfortune befell me when whelping, and now this little marble slab marks where the earth enfolds me'.

CAN YOU LEAVE ALL YOUR MONEY TO YOUR DOG IN YOUR WILL?

Despite the occasional media stories about rich celebrities or wealthy animal lovers leaving huge sums of money to a favourite cat or dog, you can't actually leave anything to a pet in your will. As far as the law is concerned, pets can't own property because they are property. Leaving your fortune to a Border Terrier is no more logical legally than leaving your pension fund to your garden or your collection of Poodle ornaments to your front room. What you can do, however, is set up a trust fund, which allows you to leave money or property to an individual or organisation on the condition that they look after your pet according to your wishes. Most pet owners worry about what might happen to their pets if they die and informal agreements between family and friends are common, but the only way to be absolutely sure that your pet will be legally protected after your death is to make it clear in your will.

GIFTS TO BATTERSEA

Around one-third of Battersea's donated income comes from gifts in wills. That's quite a sum and the Home couldn't continue without it. In fact, without wills, Battersea would probably never have got off the ground in the first place – a legacy in 1863 allowed the Home for Lost and Starving Dogs to purchase the freehold of our first centre in North London.

Battersea also runs the Forever Loved card scheme, which gives peace of mind by taking care of dogs and cats should their owners die. Battersea can take in your pet and give them all the love and care they need while we find them a loving new home.

Ten dogs memorialised

1. **The Queen's Corgis:** When Susan, the queen's first Corgi, died in 1959 she was buried near Queen Victoria's Collie at the Sandringham estate. Since then, most of the queen's many dogs have been buried in this royal pet cemetery.

2. **Station Jim:** Jim died in 1896 but he can still be seen on platform five at Slough Station. Jim collected money for the Great Western Railway Widows and Orphans Fund. He was stuffed when he died at the very tender age of two.

3. **Elgar's dogs:** The wife of composer Edward Elgar didn't like dogs, so he couldn't have one until after her death in 1920. Two of his dogs, Spaniel Marco and Cairn Terrier Mina, are buried together at the garden of the Elgar Birthplace Museum.

4. **Edith Cavell's Jack:** When British nurse, Edith Cavell, was executed by a German firing squad in 1915, her dog, Jack, was rescued by a Belgian princess. When Jack died, he was embalmed and his body is now in the Imperial War Museum's collection.

5. **Hardy's Wessex:** 'Faithful. Unflinching.' So reads the inscription on the headstone of Thomas Hardy's dog, Wessex, who died in 1926 aged 13. The Fox Terrier, who was well known for his mischievous streak, is buried at Hardy's Max Gate home in Dorset.

6. **Portmeirion pets:** The slightly incongruous Italianate village of Portmeirion in north Wales has a dog cemetery which was started by an eccentric tenant Adelaide Haig who lived in the mansion. She was also known to read sermons to her many dogs.

7. **Drummer the canine hero:** Drummer was the regimental mascot of the 1st Battalion Northumberland Fusiliers. He went to South Africa during the Boer War and was injured in the conflict. He is now stuffed and in the regimental museum at Alnwick Castle.

8. **Jacko dog detective:** When Camille Holland disappeared in 1899, suspicion fell on the man she had recently met, Samuel Dougal. Her little dog, Jacko, led the police to her body and Dougal was hanged for murder. Jacko was stuffed when he died and is now in the Essex Police Museum.

9. **The Brown Dog:** The original Brown Dog statue was unveiled in 1906 in Battersea but was removed in 1910 because the memorial to dogs who had died in medical experiments caused violent disorder between pro- and anti-vivisection campaigners. A new brown dog memorial was placed in Battersea Park in 1985.

10. **Boxer Ben:** A bronze statue of a Boxer called Ben is one of a number of tributes to dogs dotted around the Battersea buildings. The statue was created by Ben's owner, the sculptor Rudy Weller, who is best known for the four Horses of Helios in London's Piccadilly.

THE TAIL END

Dogs and humans have come a long way together since those first cautious exchanges across the species barrier many thousands of years ago when the domestication of the wolf slowly but surely turned a foe into a friend. Ever since then, our partnership has grown as the natural abilities of the dog have been honed and harnessed to help us with a remarkable range of tasks. Over many centuries, dogs have become thoroughly interwoven into the fabric of our domestic lives and their imprint is everywhere from farming methods and law enforcement to leisure pursuits and art and literature.

These days, of course, most dogs are primarily companions – a role they've largely taken to with great joy and enthusiasm. Nevertheless, despite our best intentions, humans don't always get it right when it comes to providing our canine friends with a lifestyle that puts their well-being first and foremost. They are, after all, a different species, and they experience the world from a totally different perspective. Fortunately, research into canine behaviour has come on in leaps and bounds in recent years and we're rapidly developing a better understanding of why our dogs do what they do. Around a quarter of UK households include a dog and education is the key to making sure our dogs lead contented lives in harmony with our own.

Sadly, cruelty and neglect have been as much a part of the dog's story as kindness and respect. Although legislation has done much to alleviate the suffering of animals since the days when Mary Tealby first set up the Home, there are still incidents of deliberate cruelty and casual mistreatment. Even today, the decision to get a dog is too often taken lightly and far too many puppies are bred and sold without due consideration for their long-term welfare. Battersea Dogs & Cats Home has looked after over three million animals since it opened in 1860 and this vital work will continue as long as there are dogs (and cats) in need. It's the least our ever faithful friends deserve.